John Jackson

The Witness of the Spirit

Sermons Preached before the University of Oxford

John Jackson

The Witness of the Spirit
Sermons Preached before the University of Oxford

ISBN/EAN: 9783744742306

Printed in Europe, USA, Canada, Australia, Japan

Cover: Foto ©Lupo / pixelio.de

More available books at **www.hansebooks.com**

THE

WITNESS OF THE SPIRIT:

Sermons

PREACHED BEFORE THE UNIVERSITY
OF OXFORD.

BY

JOHN JACKSON, D.D.

BISHOP OF LONDON.

THIRD EDITION.

LONDON:
WILLIAM SKEFFINGTON,
163 PICCADILLY.

1870.

CONTENTS.

SERMON I.

HAVE I THE SPIRIT OF GOD?

Romans, viii. 9.

PAGE

But ye are not in the flesh, but in the Spirit, if so be that the Spirit of God dwell in you. Now if any man have not the Spirit of Christ, he is none of His 1

SERMON II.

THE EVIDENCE OF JUSTIFICATION.

2 Cor. xiii. 5.

Examine yourselves, whether ye be in the faith; prove your ownselves: know ye not your ownselves, how that Jesus Christ is in you, except ye be reprobates? 22

SERMON III.
THE CHARACTER AND BLESSING OF THE PREDESTINATE.
Romans, viii. 28.

PAGE

And we know that all things work together for good to them that love God, to them who are the called according to his purpose 40

SERMON IV.
FAITH A GIFT OF THE SPIRIT.
1 Cor. xii. pt. 3.

No man can say that Jesus is the Lord, but by the Holy Ghost 57

SERMON V.
FAITH A GIFT OF THE SPIRIT.
Acts, xv. 8. 9.

And God, which knoweth the hearts, bare them witness, giving them the Holy Ghost, even as he did unto us; and put no difference between us and them, purifying their hearts by faith . . 76

SERMON VI.
GRACE: THE PERSONAL AGENCY OF THE HOLY SPIRIT.
Romans, viii. 14.

As many as are led by the Spirit of God, they are the sons of God . . , . . . 94

SERMON VII.

GRACE NOT A QUALITY.

1 Cor. xv. 10.

PAGE

Yet not I, but the grace of God which was with me . 114

SERMON VIII.

GIFTS GIVEN TO PROFIT WITHAL.

1 Cor. xii. 7.

But the manifestation of the Spirit is given to every man to profit withal 132

SERMON IX.

GRIEVING THE SPIRIT.

Ephes. iv. 30.

And grieve not the Holy Spirit of God, whereby ye are sealed unto the day of redemption . . 149

SERMON X.

THE DISCERNMENT OF SPIRITUAL THINGS.

1 Cor. ii. 14.

But the natural man receiveth not the things of the Spirit of God: for they are foolishness unto him: neither can he know them, because they are spiritually discerned 166

SERMON XI.

SELF-CONCEIT ITS OWN PUNISHMENT.

Romans, xii. pt. 16.

Be not wise in your own conceits 184

SERMON XII.

THE DANGERS TO THE CLERGY OF A TIME OF CONTROVERSY.

1 Tim. iv. pt. 16.

Take heed unto thyself, and unto the doctrine . . 206

ADVERTISEMENT TO THE FIRST AND SECOND EDITIONS.

The first ten Sermons in this Volume, though preached at intervals during a period of nine years, will be found to have a certain unity of subject, and to have reference mainly to some errors either of practice or opinion respecting the office and work of the Holy Spirit, which have occurred to the Author in the course of his ministry or of his reading. A Sermon was delivered between the third and fourth on "Repentance as a gift of the Holy Spirit," which would properly form part of the Series, and would have been inserted in its place, had it not been expanded in a course of Lent Lectures already published.[1] The eleventh Sermon was preached on Quinquagesima Sunday on one of the texts prescribed for that day by the terms of the benefaction of Mr. Masters: and the twelfth, though not delivered before the University, is added on account of the importance of the subject.

Rishholme, 1854.

[1] Repentance: its Necessity, Nature and Aids. Skeffington.

ADVERTISEMENT TO THE THIRD EDITION.

NEARLY a quarter of a century has passed since the earliest—more than fifteen years since the latest of these Sermons was delivered; yet they will not be found, it is hoped, inapplicable to the special circumstances and difficulties of the present day. In reading them over, when preparing them for the press, the author could not but observe how opinions and modes of thought, against which he had felt it his duty to warn those whom he addressed long since from the University pulpit, and some of which existed then in tendency rather than in system,—have since developed and spread, and have gone, on the one hand, to take their place among the doctrines of rationalism, or have assisted, on the other, to build up a theory of sacramental grace, which, however disguised from both teacher and disciple under vague and ambiguous terms, is in fact a materialistic, and therefore a low and unscriptural, view of the operations of the Holy Spirit. It will be the cause of much thankfulness and an answer to prayer, if the perusal of these Sermons should help to guide or confirm any into whose hands they fall, in the simple teaching of the word of God.

FULHAM PALACE, 1870.

SERMON I.

HAVE I THE SPIRIT OF GOD?

Romans, viii. 9.

But ye are not in the flesh, but in the Spirit, if so be that the Spirit of God dwell in you. Now if any man have not the Spirit of Christ, he is none of His.

It may well be doubted, whether times of religious excitement, like the present, are more favourable, on the whole, or injurious to the growth of personal piety. On the one hand, the attention is strongly roused; important truths are presented in striking lights, illuminated by the glow of controversy, and in action, like realities; and that torpor of the soul is rendered well-nigh impossible, in which many in quieter times hold the truth without believing it, unconscious alike of the blessings it involves and the duties it imposes. For good or evil men must think; and when they think, they may feel. And thus is a great point gained. But on the other hand, besides the unchristian tempers and the bitter spirit, which controversy too often engenders; besides the imminent danger of mistaking party spirit for religion, zeal for a truth for zeal for the God of truth; there is great peril to the soul from the objective character which truth at such times assumes. It is placed without us; something to be defended rather than felt; or if felt, felt rather as a matter of importance to others, than of all-absorbing interest to ourselves. Besides, momentous as are often the principles involved in the contest, they yet do not generally touch those awful personal questions, on the answer to which, after all, our own hopes of salvation depend, and which may remain to be answered, even when the whole circle of Christian doctrine has been discussed, defended, and grasped with all the force of the most comprehensive intellect. They do not touch them; but they may draw off the attention from them. The soul, eager and occupied, may neglect to interrogate its own state; and personal religion may suffer even in the pursuit of truth.

It is well, then, that by the recurrence of seasons like the present,[1] the Church should recall us from discussion of truths without, to the contemplation of truths within; and bidding us cease from controversy for a season,—proclaiming, as it were, a 'truce of God,'—should turn the eye of the soul inward on itself, to examine there,—as each searches by the light of God's word the record of his own consciousness,—our own sinfulness, our own dangers, our own hopes. At such times there are questions which must be asked and answered,—solemn questions, involving,

[1] Preached in Lent, 1845.

not as matters of speculation, but in personal connexion with ourselves, the favour and love of God, our own growth in iniquity or holiness, heaven and hell, the life and death of eternity. Of this character is the question implied in the text, Have I the Spirit of God?

That there must be a real indwelling of the Spirit of God in the true Christian, with the Bible before us, we can scarcely doubt. It is the distinguishing promise of the new covenant: "as God hath said, I will dwell in them, and walk in them; and I will be their God, and they shall be My people."[1] It is the fulfilment of our Saviour's words: "If a man love me, he will keep my words: and my Father will love him, and we will come unto him, and make our abode with him."[2] It is the pledge of adoption: "for as many as are led by the Spirit of God, they are the sons of God. For ye have not received the spirit of bondage again to fear; but ye have received the Spirit of adoption, whereby we cry, Abba, Father:"[3] the evidence of sonship: "because ye are sons, God hath sent the Spirit of His Son into your hearts, crying, Abba, Father:"[4] the seal of redemption by Christ: "in whom also after that ye believed, ye were sealed with that holy Spirit of promise:"[5] the earnest of glory: "which is the earnest of our inheritance until the redemption of the purchased possession."[6] It is

[1] 2 Cor. vi. 16.   [2] John, xiv. 21.   [3] Rom. viii. 14, 15.
[4] Gal. iv. 6.   [5] Eph. i. 13.   [6] Eph. i. 14.

the Shekinah of the Christian temple, the presence of Jehovah in the heart—yea, in the sanctified body —of the humble and contrite : " What, know ye not that your body is the temple of the Holy Ghost, which is in you ?"[1] It is absolutely essential, then, to our hopes of acceptance with God and salvation through Christ. " They that are in the flesh cannot please God. But ye are not in the flesh, but in the Spirit: if so be that the Spirit of God dwell in you. Now, if any man have not the Spirit of Christ he is none of His."

It is then, perhaps, the most important and awful question the soul can put to itself, Have I the Spirit of God? And it is a question, the answer to which is independent, to a great extent, of the variations of schools of doctrine. They who hold the tenets of post-baptismal regeneration and the indefectibility of grace, are bound, of course, to ask it of themselves, as the one great test which separates between the elect and the reprobate; those who are God's, and those who are not. And as those who believe that in baptism we are not merely translated from the world into the Church, and from being children of wrath are adopted to be children of grace, but also that the Holy Spirit is then given us as the principle of a new life and the seal of our adoption, admit that the Holy Spirit, thus received, may be resisted, grieved, and quenched—and *that*, not merely by our own fault, but

---
[1] 1 Cor. vi. 19.

(according to that mysterious law which links not our temporal only, but our spiritual being and wellbeing with external influence and agency), by the neglect or evil example of others, so that the pulse of life within may beat fainter and fainter, and the light wax dimmer, till " the lamp of God goes out in the temple of the Lord " and all is still ;—it follows that it is an anxious question also to them, whether they *now* (for this is the point of importance) have the Spirit of God.

Nor must it be thought that the answer is among those " secret things which belong unto the Lord our God," and which the last day only will reveal, but which it is presumption to seek for now in the confessions of our own consciousness. If the presence of the Spirit of Christ in us be " a seal," it must be distinguishable; if it be an " earnest," it must be felt and enjoyed; if it " beareth witness," it must be itself an ascertained and intelligible fact. And, therefore, our seventeenth article speaks scripturally of those who "*feel* in themselves the working of the Spirit of Christ." It may, indeed, be said, that in the miraculous gifts of the Holy Ghost Christians of the apostolic times had an evidence of the presence of the Spirit which we do not possess; so that the solemn question involved in the text might receive a definite answer from them, which can have no counterpart in our own case. It must be observed, however, in reply, that it does not appear that all believers received the extraordinary gifts of the Holy Ghost; while the evidence and earnest of the Spirit was required in all. "*If any man* have not the Spirit of Christ he is none of his." So that many of the primitive Christians,—in some churches probably the great mass,—were in possession only of spiritual privileges, the same in kind (however greater in degree in proportion to their greater faith and earnestness) with those which are still our precious heritage. Besides, it may be doubted, whether miraculous powers were a surer test of the indwelling of the Spirit than any that we possess. At least St. John warns those to whom he wrote, "not to believe every spirit, but to try the spirits whether they are of God: because many false prophets are gone out into the world."[1] And the standard by which he would have their pretensions measured, is not the power of working miracles (a power which our Lord Himself predicted would be assumed by false Christs and false prophets), but the soundness of their faith and the reality of their love. "Hereby know ye the Spirit of God: every spirit that confesseth that Jesus Christ is come in the flesh is of God: and every spirit that confesseth not that Jesus Christ is come in the flesh, is not of God. If we love one another, God dwelleth in us."[2] And St. Paul appears to intimate the possibility of speaking with the tongues of men and angels, of having the gift of prophecy and understanding all mysteries and

[1] 1 John, iv. 1.   [2] 1 John, iv. 2, 12.

all knowledge, yea, of having all faith so as to remove mountains, and yet to want the more excellent gift of the Spirit and the surest evidence of His presence, and so to be nothing.[1] Accordingly we do not find him referring his converts for the criterion of their spiritual state to their extraordinary endowments and miraculous powers, but to something within—the indwelling of Christ in their souls. "Examine yourselves, whether ye be in the faith; prove your own selves. Know ye not your own selves, how that Jesus Christ is in you, except ye be reprobates?"[2] There would seem, then, as respects the point before us, to be no material difference between the earliest believers and ourselves; and the question which the words of the text involved in their case, returns in all its solemn and unspeakable importance on each one of us individually,—Have I the Spirit of God?

It is not, of course, contended, that we have absolute and demonstrative certainty of the presence of the Holy Spirit, any more than of any other fact which depends on evidence, and consequently admits of doubt. We can have as much moral certainty as we need for practice; ground enough for hope to build and joy to flourish on. Who doubts that he is in health, when the pulse beats truly, and the nerves are braced, and the spirits buoyant, and each organ with unfelt regularity elaborates its proper functions? Questioned it may be; demonstrated it cannot be:

[1] 1 Cor. xiii. 1, 2.   [2] 2 Cor. xiii. 5.

but we know it, and are thankful. And so there may be evidence of the in-dwelling of the Spirit within us,—not demonstrative, indeed,—but sufficient to make the believer walk warily, as one who has received a precious gift which he is bound to cherish, and to fill his bosom with peace, and thankfulness, and joy of the Holy Ghost.

But what is this evidence? How is the question before us to be answered? Not, surely, by the mere possession of sacramental privileges; so that a man may say, I have been baptized, and therefore I have the Spirit; I have communicated in the Supper of the Lord, and therefore I have the Spirit. For though the sacraments be, indeed, occasions and means of grace,—holy vessels by which we draw for the soul's thirst from the Fountain of living water; though baptism be the laver of regeneration—the birthday of the spiritual life—to those who receive it in repentance and faith, performed then, or promised then and performed thereafter; and though in the Supper of the Lord the souls of the faithful receive the spiritual reality of the body and blood of Christ; yet as the one may be vitiated to all saving purposes, and the Spirit, therein covenanted, may be grieved and quenched by the non-performance of the promises then made; and the other, taken and received unworthily, may but minister to condemnation and tend to extinguish the light within us; so it is evident that the mere possession of sacramental privileges,—however precious pledges, when rightly used, of grace received,—is not, and cannot be, a safe and sufficient evidence that the Spirit of God dwelleth within us. And thus the Apostle, in the passage before us, intimates the possibility that some of those, of whom we have proof in the Epistle itself, that they were participators in both the sacraments, might yet be without the Spirit. "But ye are not in the flesh but in the Spirit, if so be (εἴπερ) the Spirit of God dwell in you. But if (εἰ δέ) any man have not the Spirit of Christ, he is none of His." And he writes to the Corinthians, who were baptized communicants, "Whereas there is among you envying, and strife, and divisions, are ye not carnal, and walk as men?"[1] So that while the possession and use of the sacraments are the badge and privilege of Christians, and separate the Church from the world; there is another and yet more important division even in the visible Church of Christ itself,—the division between the "carnally-minded" and the "spiritually-minded;" between those who "have the Spirit" and those who have not; between those "who are Christ's" and those who "are none of His."

Still less than from sacramental privileges, can the presence of the Spirit be inferred from any mere inward feelings, however vivid and delightful in themselves, or however difficult to be accounted for

[1] 1 Cor. iii. 3.

from mere natural causes. Scripture knows no such test as these. We read, indeed, of the "comfort of the Holy Ghost,"[1] "the joy of the Holy Ghost,"[2] and "the peace of God which passeth all understanding;"[3] and these are blessed realities with which the world has nothing to compare. They are the gifts of the Spirit; but they are not *in themselves* trustworthy evidences of the Spirit's presence. Scripture does not refer us to them; and they may be counterfeited. There is a comfort which error may minister to ignorance. There is a joy which enthusiasm may kindle, and even sustain. There is a peace which stills the conscience, when lulled by the opiate of some deluding doctrine, or deadened by the indulgence of habitual sin. "Satan himself is transformed into an angel of light."[4] Excited religious feeling, exalted raptures of devotion, zeal for religious truth, a partiality for religious persons and religious topics, *may* be the fruits of the Spirit, but they may spring from a far other source. "They seek me daily," said Jehovah, by the voice of His prophet, to His falsehearted people, when He bade him "Cry aloud, spare not, lift up thy voice like a trumpet, and show my people their transgression, and the house of Jacob their sins;" "They seek me daily, and *delight* to know my ways, as a nation that did righteousness, and forsook not the ordinance of their God; they

---

[1] Acts, ix. 31.   [2] 1 Thess. i. 6.   [3] Phil. iv. 7.
[4] 2 Cor. xi. 14.

ask of me the ordinances of justice: they *take delight* in approaching to God."[1]

The only true test of the presence of the Holy Spirit is its sanctifying influence on our hearts and lives. It is evidenced only by its effects. So much, indeed, would appear to be conveyed to us even by the name by which the Almighty Comforter has been pleased to reveal Himself to us in the page of His word. The SPIRIT, πνεῦμα,—the imperceptible, yet vital *breath*, which *is*, and there is life, and will, and motion; which departs, and all is cold, and senseless, and still:—the impalpable and viewless, but powerful and beneficent *wind;* now rending the rocks and laying low the forests; now purifying the stagnant air, or opening the blossoms of spring; now wafting the seeds each to its appointed place, to "take root downwards and to bear fruit upwards,— some thirty-fold, some sixty, and some an hundred." And thus it was said by our blessed Lord Himself: "The wind bloweth where it listeth, and thou hearest the sound thereof, but canst not tell whence it cometh and whither it goeth; so is every one that is born of the Spirit."[2] As the vital principle of our material frame,—which science may search for but cannot detect, and when it has dissected the members, and analysed the fluids, and untied the muscles and ganglions, and followed line by line the delicate tracery of the nerves, is forced to confess that it has

[1] Isaiah, lviii. 1, 2.   [2] John, iii. 8.

had to do but with the instruments and mechanism of the mysterious power within,—may yet be recognised by a child's intellect in the fire of the eye, the force of the arm, and the immediate certainty with which action follows on the determination of the will; so the presence of the Holy Spirit of God in the hearts of His people, though secret itself,—the presence of the Invisible—is discernible by its effects.

And its effects are HOLINESS. This is the peculiar work, and, therefore, the certain evidence, of divine power. Nature cannot imitate it, in that it is weak through the flesh. Satan would not imitate, if he could; for it is the contradiction to himself. Hypocrisy is his work often; holiness never. And, therefore, the Spirit is throughout, in Scripture, opposed to the carnal (*i. e.* the natural) mind, and the fruits of the Spirit to the works of the flesh. And while "the deeds of the body"[1]—or, as they are elsewhere termed, our "members which are upon the earth"—are defined to be "fornication, uncleanness, inordinate affection, evil concupiscence, and covetousness which is idolatry,"[2] "the fruit of the Spirit is in all goodness, and righteousness, and truth."[3] And in the whole of the passage in which the text occurs, there is a sustained contrast between the "living after the flesh," by the corrupt, worldly, selfish principles of the unchanged heart, and the "walking after

[1] Rom. viii. 13. [2] Col. iii. 5. [3] Eph. v. 9.

the Spirit," by the renewing and purifying energy of the Holy Ghost dwelling within, recreating—slowly, perhaps, but surely—the whole moral constitution, and, consequently, evidencing His presence in the growing holiness of the life.

It will not be difficult, then, to lay down certain signs by which the working of the Holy Spirit may be inferred—not with absolute certainty, indeed (and where, when both the person judging and the object judged are our own weak, fallible selves, *can* there be certainty without presumption?)—but with an assured hope—a definite, and, oh! most comfortable answer, to the solemn question,—Have I the Spirit of God?

Of these one is true repentance; not sorrow, or even remorse, merely for the *consequences* of sin, but sorrow for sin *as sin*, as an offence (and a *Christian's* offence) against God, accompanied by detestation of it, and steadfast resolutions to forsake it. This the apostle calls "godly sorrow"[1] (ἡ κατὰ Θεὸν λυπή); not only, apparently, as having God for its object, but also for its agent; as coming from Him, as well as looking to Him. And, therefore, a conviction of sin deepening into true repentance, being the work of the Holy Spirit in the heart, is an evidence, also, of the Spirit's presence there. Hence, too, is the explanation of that paradox to mere men of the world, which some are not slow to stigmatise as hypocrisy,

[1] 2 Cor. vii. 10.

and others to pity as a delusion, that the greater our advance in holiness, the deeper ever is our sense of sinfulness; that their repentance is the most earnest who seem to need it least; that the conscience is more sensitive in proportion as it is less burdened. It is, that the same Power who sanctifies, also convinces of sin, evidencing His presence by either operation alike; that the same heavenly light streams into the recesses of our hearts, disclosing the secret springs of evil and the mystery of their natural corruption, which throws its radiance over the path of the just as it "shineth more and more unto the perfect day."[1]

Faith, too, in Jesus Christ is the work, and, therefore, an evidence of the Spirit: not faith which believes (or, rather, does not disbelieve) and cares not, which is a dead faith; nor faith which believes and trembles, which is a devil's faith; nor faith which believes and trusts only, which is a self-deceiver's faith; but faith which believes, and trusts, and loves, and therefore obeys: the faith of ransomed sinners in their Saviour; of those who not only come to Christ, but take up their cross daily, and follow Him. That such faith is a grace of the Holy Spirit is clear, both from our Saviour's words, "No man can come unto me, except the Father which hath sent me draw him,"[2] and from the language of His apostle Paul, when he thus accounts for the contrast between be-

[1] Prov. iv. 18.   [2] John, vi. 44.

lievers and those "in whom the god of this world has blinded the minds of them which believe not." "For God," he says, "who commanded the light to shine out of darkness, hath shined in our hearts, to give the light of the knowledge of the glory of God in the face of Jesus Christ."[1]

Yet more surely is the Spirit's presence witnessed by love, the energy and fruit of faith, the heat of its light. God alone is the source of the love of God; and not only do "we love Him" only "because He first loved us,"[2] but that love itself must be "shed abroad in our hearts by the Holy Ghost which is given unto us."[3] "The carnal mind," indeed, "is enmity against God,"[4] shrinks from Him, shuns communion with Him. His service is a weariness, His will a hard law. We would disobey Him if we dared; we would not depart and be with Him if we could. It is not till the reconciliation effected for us by Christ, is wrought in us by the Holy Spirit; till the enmity which was destroyed on the cross, is crucified in our hearts by grace; that the flame of love burns heavenward on the altar of the Christian temple, the gift at once and evidence of the Deity within.

And thus, too, charity—the love of our brethren, —is a grace—rather *the* grace—of the Spirit, and an index, therefore, of His power in the breast; that charity of which the apostle has drawn the beautiful

[1] 2 Cor. iv. 4, 6 [2] 1 John, iv. 19. [3] Rom. v. 5. [4] Rom. viii. 7.

lineaments with the pen of inspiration, to be, at the same time, the measure of our deficiences and the model of our endeavours.[1] And so, too, is the growing habit and power of self-denial; for it is written, "If ye, through the Spirit, do mortify the deeds of the body, ye shall live."[2] And, therefore, our 17th Article speaks of "such as feel in themselves the working of the Spirit of Christ, mortifying the works of the flesh and their earthly members." And as selfdenial is the arm, so to speak, by which the warfare of the Spirit against the flesh is waged within us, so by the ease, extent, and certainty with which the corrupt will is checked and mortified, may be gauged, to some extent, the success of the conflict and the hope of the crown.

But it is unnecessary to trace further the fount of divine grace through the various channels of Christian holiness. The fruits, and therefore evidences, of the Spirit are enumerated by His own guidance in the words of St. Paul,—"Love, joy, peace, long-suffering, gentleness, goodness, faith, meekness, temperance."[3] These are the virtues which, combined in due degree, and habitually exercised, are healthy indications of the spiritual life within.

It deserves, however, to be considered, that it is not enough that the graces of the Spirit should *be*, —they should be growing. It is at this point that the analogy between the natural and the spiritual life

[1] 1 Cor. xiii.   [2] Rom. viii. 13.   [3] Gal. v. 22, 23.

ceases. The one has its birth, its growth, its maturity, and its decay. The other, once begun, should be a perpetual progress,—with checks, no doubt, at times, and even occasional loss of ground, on account of the weakness of our nature,—but still a progress; so that from month to month and year to year, our repentance may be deeper, and our faith firmer, and our love purer, and our charity more real, and self more subject to the Spirit, and our holiness more consistent, habitual, and unwavering, even to the last day of our probation, if not, also, throughout the eternity of our glory. The life of the Spirit is a pilgrimage, a race, a warfare. Not to advance betokens the soul diseased; to loiter is to lose. And it is the divine law of all spiritual gifts—yea, of the sum and substance of all spiritual gifts, the gift of the Holy Spirit itself: " Unto every one that hath shall be given, and he shall have abundance; but from him that hath not, shall be taken away even that which he hath."[1]

And now, brethren, if it is a question which may be answered,—Have I the Spirit of God? it is surely one which we should endeavour to answer at once. The reply involves our present safety, and our hopes of a glorious eternity; for " if any man have not the Spirit of Christ, he is none of his." And if the answer is to be found in the sincerity of our repentance, the liveliness of our faith, the growth of our love, and charity, and self-denying habits,—in a word, in our

[1] Matt. xxv. 29.

progress in holiness,—ought we to allow this Lent to close without instituting a searching investigation into the state of our hearts and lives? It may be that the process may be humiliating and painful, and that some of us may stand appalled at the extent of our own poverty; the pulse of the soul's life may be beating very low, and the light of the Spirit well-nigh extinct within us. But how much happier to learn our danger now, than only to be awakened to it by the same voice which tells that our trial is over, and that hope is past. Now, repentance is permitted us, and pardon offered us, and the means of grace are yet within our reach. And if we need encouragement, we may find it in the promises of God, and the love of Him who died for sinners, and that merciful condescension which deigned to reason with His wayward creatures, if, perchance, He might persuade them to seek that best of gifts, which is so infinitely beyond their deserts, yet to want which is ruin. "If ye, then, being evil," said He who promised and who sent the Comforter, " know how to give good gifts unto your children, how much more shall your heavenly Father give the Holy Spirit to them that ask Him."[1]

But, indeed, the investigation is very necessary for all; for who is not living below his privileges and his duties? Who among us is not too slow to stir up the gift of God which is in him, even if he does not grieve

[1] Luke, xi. 13.

the Spirit by self-indulgence and sin? Who among us is anxiously keeping his soul and body pure of all offence, as the shrine of the Spirit, the temple of the Holy One of Israel? It may be that the arts of covetousness are not there—" the tables of the moneychangers;" it may be that no strange fire is burning upon the altar—the fire of hatred or of lust: but let us search and see whether there be no idols worshipped within, in the chambers of the soul's imagery,—ease, or pleasure, or self, or the world's opinion and praise, or even the excess of what we may and ought to love; unhallowing, each in their degree, the dwelling-place of the Holy Ghost; casting their hurtful shadows between us and the light of God's countenance; and dwarfing, therefore, and blighting our growth in holiness, and our fitness for heaven?

If, after all, we receive an answer of hope and peace, and are enabled humbly to trust that we are walking, not after the flesh, but after the Spirit, it will be our care to improve the precious talent committed to us by stricter watchfulness and self-control, by the careful avoidance (as far as is consistent with duty) of all occasions and inlets of temptation, and by earnest efforts after higher degrees of holiness. Every thought of evil, we shall remember, every outbreak of temper, every ungoverned word, every strain, however slight, put upon the conscience to accommodate it to the maxims or habits of the world, grieves the holy Inmate, and darkens our souls. And we shall learn to value and employ the means of grace entrusted to us, not only in obedience to the commands of God, but as the food of our soul's life, the fresh springs of our earthly pilgrimage, the refreshment of our spiritual health and strength.

And how heartfelt and fervent should be our thanksgiving to God for this most precious of His many precious gifts. That we, who were born in sin and shapen in iniquity, having been regenerated, should daily be renewed by His Holy Spirit; that we, who were aliens and enemies, should be admitted into His family, receiving "the Spirit of adoption," whereby we may cry, with childlike confidence, "Abba, Father!" that we, who were condemned and hopeless, should bear about in us the pledge of redeeming love, the seal of His grace; that we, whose doom was the doom of sinners, should be comforted in this our time of trial with the earnest of a glorious inheritance "until the redemption of the purchased possession;" that our whole moral nature, distorted as it was and shattered by the fall, should be "renewed after the image of Him that created us;" and that our bodies even,—these frail fabrics of clay, but dignified now and sanctified by the assumption of our nature by Him who "is over all God blessed for ever,"—by being made the temples of the Holy Ghost, should become the dwelling-place of the high and lofty One that inhabiteth eternity: these are mercies under the weight of which language fails, and the mind staggers bewildered. We must *act* our thanks now, that we may *speak* them throughout eternity. "I beseech you therefore, brethren,"—and many, I trust, there are who feel in themselves the working of the Spirit of Christ mortifying the works of the flesh and their earthly members, and drawing up their mind to high and heavenly things,—"I beseech you by the mercies of God, that ye present" yourselves, your souls and "bodies, a living sacrifice, holy, acceptable unto God, which is your reasonable service." [1]

[1] Rom. xii. 1.

SERMON II.

THE EVIDENCE OF JUSTIFICATION.

2 COR. xiii. 5.

Examine yourselves, whether ye be in the faith; prove your ownselves: know ye not your ownselves, how that Jesus Christ is in you, except ye be reprobates?

WHEN the soul of man seriously examines its relations towards God and its prospect of eternity, there are two questions to which it urgently desires an answer:—The first is that of Bildad, "How can man be justified with God?"[1] the second, how may we know, or (which is the knowledge of faith) how may we have a reasonable hope, that we are justified with God? The two have been confounded in discussion; but the doubting soul, burdened with a sense of sin, or pondering on the destinies of the everlasting future, will not be at peace without an answer to both.

The answer to the former question may, of course, be assumed in this place to be the one authoritatively determined by our Church: "We are accounted righteous before God, only for the merit of our

[1] Job, xxv. 4.

Lord and Saviour Jesus Christ by faith, and not for our own works and deservings;"[1] or, as it is more fully explained in the Homily to which the Article refers us; "Justification is the office of God only, and is not a thing which we render unto Him, but which we receive of Him; not which we give to Him, but which we take of Him, by His free mercy, and by the only merits of His most dearly beloved Son, our only Redeemer, Saviour, and Justifier, Jesus Christ: so that the true understanding of this doctrine, we be justified freely by faith without works, or that we be justified by faith in Christ only, is not, that this our own act to believe in Christ, or this our faith in Christ which is in us, doth justify us, and deserve our justification unto us; (for that were to count ourselves to be justified by some act or virtue that is within ourselves;) but the true understanding and meaning thereof is, that although we hear God's word and believe it; although we have faith, hope, charity, repentance, dread, and fear of God within us, and do never so many works thereunto; yet we must renounce the merit of all our said virtues, of faith, hope, charity, and all other virtues and good deeds, which we either have done, shall do, or can do, as things that be far too weak, and insufficient, and unperfect, to deserve remission of our sins and justification; and therefore we must trust only in God's mercy, and that sacrifice which our

[1] Art. XI.

High Priest and Saviour Christ Jesus, Son of God, once offered for us upon the cross, to obtain thereby God's grace and remission as well of our original sin in baptism and of all actual sin committed by us after our baptism, if we truly repent and turn unfeignedly to Him again." [1]

But if the office of justifying is God's, not ours; if He is the giver, we merely receivers of the gift; the second question becomes of unspeakable importance, How may we trust that we have received the gift—that we are justified?

The reply is frequently this: God's offers of acceptance in Christ are free and full; we have but to accept them. If, then, we have closed with His offers, and have claimed as our own Christ's imputed righteousness, we are justified. In other words, the evidence of our acceptance with God is the strength of our conviction that we are accepted. The consequences of this doctrine are such as many who teach it would be the first to repudiate. It is true, that justification is the free gift of God to undeserving man, and that faith is the hand which receives and appropriates the offered righteousness of Christ. And it is true, that the penitent soul, looking to Jesus as the propitiation for all sin, may and ought to rest all its hopes in humble confidence on Him for pardon, acceptance, and glory. But it is not true, that such confidence, however well grounded, is the proof that we are ac-

[1] Homily, " Of the Salvation of Man."

cepted. Faith is the condition, not the evidence, of justification. Faith brought to Christ the lame, the blind, and the dying; and "Go in peace" were the Saviour's gracious words, "Thy faith hath made thee whole." But the evidence of the cure thus wrought, was not the trusting hope which led them to Him, but the buoyant step, the eye kindling into meaning, and the frame invigorated with the glow and pulse of health.

But further; the faith that justifies is not simply a firm persuasion, but a firm persuasion of *the truth*. But error may be held as firmly; and the confidence built upon it; may be a strong edifice on a sandy foundation. We may have closed with God's offers after interpreting them by our own wishes, not by His word. The antinomian may say and feel, that he has claimed as his own Christ's imputed righteousness, and "continue in sin that grace may abound."[1] And if the strength of our conviction of our acceptance with God is the evidence of our acceptance, then may he who, having enrolled himself among the elect, thanks God that he is not as other men are, go down to his house justified rather than the humble penitent, who "smites upon his breast, saying, God be merciful to me a sinner."

It is said, indeed, by those who maintain the opinion we are examining, that it is only a *real* faith of which it holds, and that the faith of the antinomian

[1] Rom. vi. 1.

is but a counterfeit. And this is true. But then the difficulty recurs : How can we determine the real from the false ? If we have closed with God's offers, but may have closed in a mistaken and groundless confidence, how may the soul trust that it is justified with God ?

There is another answer which may satisfy those who are not in earnest, but which will fade from the fixed gaze of those who need, and are seeking, some solid ground of comfort. " We were justified at baptism; and, therefore, while we continue in the communion of the Church, are justified still." Here the evidence is our sacramental privileges, something tangible and definite, and professing to be, what indeed they are, pledges of God's love and good-will towards us. Were they scriptural evidence they must be admitted to be real. Now, it is not necessary to enter into the question of justification at baptism when received in infancy, though it may well be doubted whether the *term* justification is ever found in Scripture, excepting in connection with the personal faith of the person justified. It must, however, be admitted that infants, when regenerated into God's family, are placed federally in a state of acceptance with Him; and as far as this state may be expressed by the word justification, so far may our baptism be an evidence that we were then justified. But as baptism is the seal of a covenant, of which repentance and faith were the conditions stipulated on our part, it follows that, where these conditions are not performed, and a lively faith does not fulfil the engagement of the baptismal vow, the state of acceptance is lost; our iniquities have again separated between us and our God; and if justified once, we are justified no longer. It need hardly be added, that the sacrament of the Lord's Supper, though the rite in which the penitent believer realises his reconciliation to God through Christ, cannot, where the conditions on our part are wanting, either continue us in, or restore us to, a state of justification. It is admitted on all hands, that the sacrament of the body and blood of Jesus Christ received unworthily does but increase our condemnation. The doctrine of sacramental justification, then, if admitted, will not enable the anxious soul to solve the question of its own acceptance, but sends him back to himself for a response. Nothing external can. All ordinances, rites, sacraments, are vivified but by the life within. As "he was not a Jew which was one outwardly, neither was that circumcision which was outward in the flesh;"[1] so the reality of the Christian's hopes is to be found in the inward man, not in external privilege; and baptism that doth save, is "not the putting away the filth of the flesh, but the answer of a good conscience towards God."[2]

There are, indeed, those who think, that we ought

[1] Rom. ii. 28.   [2] 1 Pet. iii. 21.

not to seek an answer to the question before us, but to be content to "work out our own salvation with fear and trembling," leaving the assurance of our justification to the revelation of the judgment-day. And it is true, that a secure confidence is as unscriptural as it is detrimental to growth in holiness; and that it is vouchsafed ordinarily only to the tried soldier of Jesus Christ, when he has fought the good fight, finished his course, and kept the faith, to be able to look with undoubting eye on the crown of righteousness already laid up for him in heaven. But it is one thing to have an assurance of final salvation; and another to have a reasonable belief that we are now in a state of acceptance with God. And without such a belief, what room is there for the peace and joy which are the characteristic blessings of the Gospel? How can the Christian "serve God without fear," rejoice in the Lord always, yea, even in this world's sorrow be always rejoicing, if the weight of sin, perhaps unpardoned, is upon him, and he knows not whether the eye of God is on him in anger or in love? With the apostle the *fact* of justification is the *ground* of peace and joy. "Being justified (having been justified) by faith, we have peace with God through our Lord Jesus Christ; by whom also we have access by faith into this grace (or state of grace) wherein we stand, and rejoice in hope of the glory of God."[1] And

[1] Rom. v. 1, 2.

a trusting belief of acceptance through Christ is not so much exhibited as a privilege, as enjoined as a duty. " Let us draw near with a true heart, in full assurance of faith, having our hearts sprinkled from an evil conscience, and our bodies washed with pure water." " Cast not away, therefore, your confidence, which hath great recompense of reward."[1] It is not the Christian's part to be high-minded, but to fear. Earnest heed must he take, lest " there be in him an evil heart of unbelief in departing from the living God, and lest he be hardened by the deceitfulness of sin."[2] He must be watchful, steadfast, full of prayer. But he need not, he ought not, to " drag doubt's galling chain ;" but looking for the living evidence of his justification within him, the pledge at once of his acceptance and the witness of his adoption, no longer with the forced obedience of a slave, but with the affectionate confidence of a son, to " serve God without fear in holiness and righteousness before Him all the days of his life."[3]

The evidence of our justification is the indwelling of the Holy Spirit. "There is now no condemnation to them which are in Christ Jesus, who walk not after the flesh, but after the Spirit."[4] And if it be held that this last clause is an interpolation, it must at least be admitted to be a logical consequence from the

---

[1] Heb. x. 22, 35. [2] Heb. iii. 12, 13.
[3] Luke, i. 74, 75. [4] Rom. viii. 1.

apostle's subsequent words ; in which he contrasts the carnal mind, which is enmity against God, and consequently under condemnation (for " to be carnally-minded is death"), with the " spiritual mind, which is life and peace. They that are in the flesh," he continues, " cannot please God," and are, therefore, not in a state of justification. " But ye are not in the flesh, but in the Spirit, if so be that the Spirit of God dwell in you." The indwelling, then, of the Spirit is the evidence that we are not in the flesh, no longer, therefore, at enmity against God, no longer under condemnation ; in other words, justified.

The same truth is, I believe, expressed in the words of the text. " Examine yourselves, whether ye be in the faith ; prove your ownselves ; know ye not your ownselves, how that Jesus Christ is in you, except ye be reprobates ?" It is true that many expositors from whom it seems presumptuous to differ, apply these words to the existence of miraculous powers in the Corinthian Church ; as if the apostle's meaning was, Examine yourselves whether ye be still in the faith, by testing whether the power of working miracles still remains among you. Do you not know that Jesus Christ is still in your Church by the extraordinary gifts which He bestows, unless, examined by this test and failing in the trial, you are found to be reprobates ? But it must be remembered, that these words are addressed to the same Church, which we find, but a few months before, enjoying in great abundance the miraculous gifts of the Spirit; which, indeed, were bestowed so liberally, that its members were betrayed into an uncharitable emulation by the comparison of their several endowments, or disturbed the order and decency of public worship by their display. It can hardly be conceived that such gifts could have been lost so speedily or their exercise so unaccountably neglected, as to render it necessary to exhort the Corinthians to try whether miraculous powers still remained among them. Their fault was, that they prided themselves on the possession of the extraordinary gifts, and they were more in danger of exerting them unjustifiably, than of undervaluing and forgetting them. Nor, indeed, is it at all certain, that the possession of the *miraculous* powers would prove the possessors not reprobates. At the last day, at least, "many will say unto me," said our blessed Saviour, " Lord, Lord, have we not prophesied in thy name? and in thy name have cast out devils? and in thy name done many wonderful works? And then will I profess unto them, I never knew you : depart from me ye that work iniquity."[1]

It is probable that this exposition has been adopted from not observing a peculiarity, by no means unfrequent in St. Paul's style; that when he has used a figure or certain form of expression in one application, he is led on (as by an ardent mind full of an idea) to employ it in a somewhat different application

[1] Matt. vii. 22, 23.

to the next step in his series of thought. Thus, in this same epistle we read, "Do we begin again to commend ourselves? or need we, as some others, epistles of recommendation from you? Ye are our epistle written in our hearts, known and read of all men: forasmuch as ye are manifestly declared to be the epistle of Christ, ministered by us, written not with ink, but with the Spirit of the living God; not in tables of stone, but in fleshly tables of the heart." [1] Where, first, the conversion of the Corinthians is St. Paul's letters commendatory; then they are, as it were, a letter written by Christ, the administration of which is committed to Paul; then the Gospel, which constitutes them such, is written, not as the law on tables of stone, but by the Spirit on the tables of the heart; an idea, which is thenceforth the keynote, as it were, of the remainder of the chapter. And so in the passage before us. St. Paul does, indeed, speak of the miraculous power of punishing the Corinthians for disobedience, as the mark of his apostleship; and implies that the absence of it would prove him reprobate; though he hopes that their return to obedience will render it unnecessary for him to put it to the test. "But I trust," he says, "that ye shall know that we are not reprobates. Now, I pray to God that ye do no evil; not that we should appear approved, but that ye should do that which is honest, though we be as

[1] 2 Cor. iii. 1—3.

reprobates. For we can do nothing against the truth, but for the truth." But the test of *their* state, according to which they would require, or not require, that chastisement, the power of inflicting which was an inseparable attribute of true apostleship, was not the gift of miracles, of which (at that time, at least) they could not be ignorant, but the indwelling of the Spirit of Christ. By this criterion he desires them to judge themselves, that he, as God's minister, may not judge them. " Examine yourselves, whether ye be in the faith; prove your own selves. Know ye not your own selves, how that Jesus Christ is in you, except ye be reprobates?" They, then, are rejected, not accepted; reprobate, not justified, in whom Christ is not. And Christ is in His people by His Spirit, whom He sends from the Father. " I will pray the Father," He said, " and He shall give you another Comforter, that He may abide with you for ever, even the Spirit of truth;" and adds, repeating the same promise in other words: " I will not leave you comfortless; I will come to you." [1]

The evidence of man's justification, then, is the indwelling of the Holy Spirit in the heart,—discernible (as alone the presence of the invisible Sanctifier can be discerned), by repentance, faith, and love, and growth in holiness. And if we would have a reasonable hope that our sins are blotted out in the Saviour's blood, the sentence against us cancelled,

[1] John, xiv. 16—18.

and the light of God's countenance beaming upon us in love, we must read the blessed truth in our growing hatred of sin, our increasing conformity to the example of Christ, and our strengthening habits of devotion, self-denial, purity, humility, and charity. Sanctification, as it always accompanies, becomes the outward manifestation of our justification; God's seal on those who are His. When our hearts, where an unsparing repentance has broken down the idols they enshrined, have been cleansed by the blood of sprinkling, they must become temples of the Holy Ghost, habitations of God by His Spirit. Unless He dwell there, enlightening, purifying, vivifying by His presence, there may have been glimpses indeed of His favour, and a short-lived comfort; but the heart, not in earnest, and therefore unchanged, will soon be occupied again by its ejected sins; the light of God's countenance will be withdrawn; and "the unclean spirit, returning to his house and finding it empty, will take with him seven other spirits, more wicked than himself, and they will enter in and dwell there: and the last state of that man is worse than the first." [1]

It is urged as an objection to the doctrine thus stated, that it rests our hopes of acceptance with God on the sandy foundation of man's good works, instead of on the rock of Christ's merits and God's faithfulness. If, however, it is meant that man's works are

[1] Matt. xii. 44, 45.

made in any sense the cause or condition of justification, the charge is false. We are justified, as sinners deserving nothing but condemnation,—unprofitable servants, if we had done all,—wicked and slothful servants, because we have done less than is commanded us,—only by God's free mercy, for the merits of our Lord and Saviour Jesus Christ, by faith. This is the foundation of the Christian's every hope of acceptance here, and of glory hereafter. But if it is meant that our hopes of our own acceptance must be stronger or weaker in proportion as we find the evidence of our justification in the growth or decay of the fruits of the Spirit—our progress or declension in holiness,—it is, indeed, true. But the objection cannot be urged, without objecting at the same time to our Lord's teaching and the general language of Scripture. Our hopes *are* made to depend on our practice. It is not merely in judging of others that our rule is to be, " By their fruits ye shall know them." In ourselves, obedience,—not feeling, not privilege, not even a self-renouncing reliance on the faithfulness of God's promises,—is proposed as the test. It was *doing* our Saviour's words which constituted the difference between him who built his house on the rock and him who built on sand. It is doing the will of our Father which is in heaven, which has the promise of admission into His kingdom.[1] And in every intimation of the procedure of the judgment-day

[1] See Matt. vii. 21—29.

given us by the Great Judge Himself, it is works, not faith alone, which are then to weigh in the balance: the lamps trimmed and burning, the servant employed in his master's house, the improvement of our talents, acts of kindness done or not done, to the least of Christ's brethren for His sake. The fruits of the Spirit will be the evidence by which we shall be sentenced then; the fruits of the Spirit are the evidence of our justification now. And it is no objection to the doctrine before us, but rather its corroboration by its correspondence with the word of God, that it makes our hopes of acceptance and peace with God weaker or stronger in proportion to our subjection to sin or our growth in holiness. There *is* no hope—no *scriptural* hope—for the unholy. But there is joy and peace in believing; there is a happiness well worth the exercise and training in having a conscience void of offence towards God and towards men; there is a secret reward within for every self-denying effort for God's sake; there is a calm and comfort on the death-bed in the retrospect of a life spent in God's service;—not because there is merit in any or all of these to purchase our acceptance with God, or endure the severity of His judgment, but because they are the fruits of the indwelling Spirit, which is the evidence of our justification, the pledge of our adoption, and the earnest of our glory.

To call such happy confidence of God's favour thus grounded, self-righteousness, is to confound terms.

Self-righteousness is a want of a sense of unworthiness, of true humility, which is the very groundwork of holiness. Conviction of sin, with the consequent renunciation of all merit in the sight of God, is one of the earliest creations of the Spirit in the heart. Where, then, a true, deep humility does not exist, there is not the evidence of the Spirit; where it does, there is not self-righteousness. The union, indeed, of distrust of self with trust in God,—the sense of demerit, coupled with a happy consciousness of God's work in us, is one of the paradoxes of the Christian character. It is strongly exemplified in St. Paul. In himself, the chief of sinners;[1] in God, he proposes himself to his converts as the pattern of a holy walk and conversation.[2] In himself, "not meet to be called an apostle;"[3] in God, he was "not a whit behind the very chiefest apostles,"[4] but "laboured more abundantly than they all."[5] "Not sufficient of himself to think anything as of himself,"[6] he could "do all things through Christ that strengthened him."[7] At one while he "keeps under his body and brings it into subjection, lest that by any means, when he had preached to others, he himself should be a castaway;"[8] at another, "he is persuaded that neither death, nor life, nor angels, nor principalities, nor powers, nor things present, nor

---

[1] 1 Tim. i. 15.
[2] 1 Cor. iv. 16; xi. 1.
[3] 1 Cor. xv. 9.
[4] 2 Cor. xi. 5.
[5] 1 Cor. xv. 10.
[6] 2 Cor. iii. 5.
[7] Phil. iv. 13.
[8] 1 Cor. ix. 27.

things to come, nor height, nor depth, nor any other creature, shall be able to separate us from the love of God, which is in Christ Jesus our Lord."[1] This is not presumption: rather, it is the strength of human weakness when resting on the Divine power. It is not inconsistency: rather, the humility which prompts the one feeling, is the evidence which justifies the other. Where the Spirit of Christ is, there is conviction of sin, self-renunciation, self-distrust; and where these habits prove the presence of the Spirit of Christ, there we may humbly, joyfully hope that we are yet in the faith, are justified and accepted with God.

Two lessons, then, result. First, that when the soul, burdened with a sense of guilt and anxiously revolving the solemn question, "What must I do to be saved?" has betaken itself (as in the Gospel it is invited and entreated to do), to the mercy of God in Christ; it may not rest satisfied (however, it may hope in His promises), that it is pardoned, accepted, accounted righteous before God, till in deeper repentance, firmer faith, warmer love, more earnest, cheerful, self-denying obedience, it has the evidence of the indwelling of the Spirit, the seal that God sets on those whom He has made His. It is not the mere consciousness of having closed with God's offers; it is not the privileges of our baptism and our election into the visible Church; it is nothing but our growth

[1] Rom. viii. 38, 39.

in holiness, the manifestation of the sanctifying power within,— imperfect, indeed, sadly imperfect and intermittent, but yet real,—which should be allowed to speak to us of the joy and peace of believing, of the calm of a cleansed conscience, and the happiness of a soul at peace with God.

And if so, secondly, how earnest should we be that the witness may speak clearly and intelligibly; how watchful against sin, how jealous of self, how fearful lest we grieve or quench the Spirit, how diligent in the use of all the means of grace, how unwearied in every good work. God has pardoned us in Christ that we may serve Him: let us serve Him, that we may have a reasonable hope that He has pardoned us. Christ is in us, except we be reprobates; let us, therefore, "love Christ" and "keep His commandments," that "He and His Father may come unto us and make their abode with us."[1] There is now "no condemnation to them which are in Christ Jesus;" they are justified freely by His blood, and have the enjoyment of present peace and the hope of future glory. Oh, let us strive and pray, then, to walk not after the flesh, but after the Spirit: for "if any man have not the Spirit of Christ, he is none of His."

[1] John, xiv. 23.

ND
SERMON III.

THE CHARACTER AND BLESSING OF THE PREDESTINATE.

ROMANS, viii. 28.

And we know that all things work together for good to them that love God, to them who are the called according to his purpose.

THERE is nothing so humbling to the pride of the human intellect as an attempt to comprehend the nature or trace the purposes of the Deity. His creation He has spread out before us to study and admire; and has endowed us with faculties to analyse and group its parts, to detect the laws by which it is governed, and even to modify and remodel the combinations of its elements, so as to increase our power and multiply our enjoyments. It is an inexhaustible field, indeed, but fertile. New truths are continually brought to light. One fact leads to another; and each discovery opens the way to some further recess of nature's mysteries. And men are intoxicated with repeated draughts of knowledge: and as one stronghold after another falls before their attacks, and the realm of science is perpetually extended; as the powers of the material world grow pliant in their grasp, and yield to be the obedient ministers of their will; as they disentangle by laborious reasonings the mechanism of the heavens, and count the worlds and measure the systems which roll through their boundless extent, they exult in the might of their own intellect, and feel almost as if the promise of the tempter were realized, and they were become as gods, knowing good and evil. But when we turn our thoughts on the Creator Himself, how soon the grasp of the mind fails. He is infinite: what *is* infinity? The idea is too vast for us: it retreats before us as we pursue it in thought throughout the realms of space, till we are forced to stop, and content ourselves with a negative notion:—infinity must be, because there can be no bounds. He is omnipresent: how can He be everywhere, and yet not every thing?—filling infinity, yet everywhere perfect and the same? He is eternal: how could He have no beginning? how no ending? Yet how can it be otherwise? Succession is impossible with Him; the future and the past are alike present. How *can* this be, which yet *must* be? Here the mind fails, overpowered by conceptions it cannot contain. Here the weakness of human intellect stands confessed, when brought before the presence of the Deity. And at times, when it has presumptuously striven to grapple with these great ideas and the questions to which they lead, the powers of the mind have broken overstrained by the attempt; or the process has ended in conducting the dizzy reasoner to some revolting absurdity or glaring contradiction.

And so it is, when the nature and attributes of God come in contact, as it were, with the will and acts of men. Questions arise which we are not competent now to solve. Omniscient, He must know all that will be, and all, therefore, that we shall do. Omnipotent, our wills must be subordinate to His, and every voluntary action, as well as all external events, must be ordained or foreknown by Him. And the foreknowledge of omnipotence seems in itself a kind of law; permissive, where not compulsory. That which without Him could not be, depends upon His will. He may not be its author—if it is evil, He *cannot* be its author; but its author without Him would be powerless. He may not will it *to be;* but He wills that it *may be;* and *it is.* And thus, ordained or permitted, all possible events seem bounded and defined within the limits of Almighty Omniscience. And yet our will is free. Reason concludes it; consciousness knows it; revelation implies it. Our temporal and eternal destinies must be in His hands; and yet we have in our own power the alternatives of good and evil, happiness and misery. Reconcile these truths, with our present faculties we cannot. Yet truths they are, and capable of proof on the same grounds on which our firmest convictions rest; and to deny either of them involves the reasoner in difficulties far greater than to let them stand side by side, irreconcileable perhaps now, but each a certain, independent truth. The note may be struck hereafter which will blend these discords into harmony.

Questions such as these Scripture does not solve. It states the truths: it does not teach us how they coexist. Still they are among the secret things which belong unto the Lord our God. And, perhaps, one of the most fruitful sources of error is the attempt to reconcile what revelation has not reconciled. Men would unlock the mysteries of heaven with keys of their own forging and of earthly temper. They would track and complete the circle of God's designs, of which He has shown us but a few detached segments. They would have a system of theology, compact, definite, and harmonious; and they have one; but it is their own, not God's. This is the history of Calvinism, Socinianism, and much of Romanism. The word of God leaves many voids in the metaphysical unity of His revelations. Many questions, which reason cannot solve, are not solved there. But this it does:—It deduces from each all that practically concerns ourselves, and leaves no truth obscure in its bearings on our faith and duties. There may be limits as to what we know. None can plead ignorance of what they have to do.

Such is the case with the doctrines of God's predestination and man's free will. It would seem to be the conclusion of reason no less than the revelation of Scripture, which is thus stated in our 17th

Article: "Predestination to life is the everlasting purpose of God, whereby (before the foundations of the world were laid) he hath constantly decreed by his counsel, secret to us, to deliver from curse and damnation those whom he hath chosen in Christ out of mankind, and to bring them by Christ to everlasting salvation, as vessels made to honour." And yet it is no less true, that salvation has been purchased for all, and is offered to all; that the grace of the Holy Spirit is promised to all who seek it; that two ways are set before all of us,—the narrow way which leadeth unto life, and the broad path which leadeth to destruction: that only those will be saved, and all those, who strive to enter in at the strait gate, and work out their own salvation with fear and trembling. We cannot reconcile these truths. But if we could, —if we had the hidden doctrine which could combine God's predestination and eternal calling with man's efforts, choice, and probation,—we should have no whit more certainty given to our hopes; no whit more clearness added to our duty. For all practical purposes we should have gained nothing. Now,— and it could be no more,—" the godly consideration of predestination and our election in Christ is full of sweet, pleasant, and unspeakable comfort to godly persons, and such as feel in themselves the working of the Spirit of Christ mortifying the works of the flesh and their earthly members, and drawing up their mind to high and heavenly things." And now, *of the Predestinate.* 45

the offers of the Gospel are made freely and fully to us all, and we are commanded with a distinctness, to which no greater knowledge could add either clearness or stringency, to "give diligence to make our calling and election sure."[1]

Nor is there any practical difficulty (further than belongs to self-knowledge in general) in answering that all-important question, Whether we may trust to be among the predestinated to life. We need not dive into the deep counsels of God; we need not yearn to read that mysterious roll in which is inscribed the catalogue of the saints of the most High. The decree of God's purpose is written on man's heart; and the inscription is HOLINESS. Such is evidently the teaching of the text: "We know that all things work together for good to them that love God, to them that are the called according to his purpose." The called according to His purpose are those who "love Him,"—who have within them the constraining motive of all obedience, the life of religion and well-spring of charity,—that first and great commandment, which those who keep are His, and those who do not, are Christians but in name.

To the same effect the Apostle continues in the succeeding verse: "For whom he did foreknow, he also did predestinate to be conformed to the image of His Son, that he might be the first-born among many brethren." Those who are predestinated, are

[1] 2 Pet. i. 10.

predestinated to be conformed to the image of Christ: and the lineaments of his character in ourselves is the test to judge whether God's purpose is being fulfilled in us. There must be a growing likeness to Him who, in the family of God, is "the firstborn among many brethren," before we can have a good hope that we are chosen (in anything but title) to be "heirs of God and joint-heirs with Christ." In a word, "the foundation of God standeth sure, having this seal, The Lord knoweth them that are His:" and this He alone can read: but there is another part of the inscription legible to all; "Let every one that nameth the name of Christ depart from iniquity."[1]

If, then, there be any who listen perplexedly to such passages of holy writ as those to which we have referred, in which God's predestination and eternal purpose are linked with the salvation of man, and unquiet questions arise in their breasts, which some foster into alarm or even despair, and others turn from impatiently, and hear with dislike and almost anger the doctrines named from which such questions spring,—let me recall you from them, my brethren, to the question involved in the text, which (whatever theoretical and abstract problems may yet remain unsolved) will free the subject from all *practical* difficulties, and enable you (if you will) to plant your feet on a hope that will not fail, and even to draw consolation from truths which are your discomfort

[1] 2 Tim. ii. 19.

now. "We know that all things work together for good to them that love God, to them who are the called according to his purpose." The called according to His purpose are they who love Him. Do you then love Him? Are your hearts drawn towards Him by a sense of His love, His goodness, His greatness, His manifold perfections? Especially do your affections kindle towards Him as your Redeemer,—the Father who spared not His own Son, but delivered Him up for you; the Son who emptied Himself of His glory, lived for you in lowliness, and died for you in agony and shame; the Holy Ghost who dwells in you, re-creates you, sanctifies you, a temple for God, a vessel meet for heaven? Do you love to meditate on Him, to recount His mercies, to commune with Him in prayer, to hear Him in His word, to meet Him in His Church, to seek a closer union with Him in His Sacraments? Above all (for true love "loves not in word, neither in tongue, but in deed and in truth"[1]) do you dedicate yourselves sincerely to His service? Are you anxious and watchful to do His will? Do you guard carefully against whatever may displease Him? Are you desirous to sacrifice every sin to Him, every indulgence which interferes with His supremacy in the heart? Are you seeking and praying for higher degrees of grace and holiness, and endeavouring to love and do good to those about you, because they are His, and He loves them too?

[1] 1 John, iii. 18.

In a word, instead of "the spirit of bondage again to fear," have you "received the Spirit of adoption whereby you cry Abba, Father; the Spirit itself bearing witness with your spirit that you are the children of God?"[1] If so, what matters it whether you can reconcile metaphysically the predestination of God with the free will of man? You have chosen the good part; and He has predestinated, called, justified, sanctified you. You have His seal, and are His; and what shall separate you from Him? "He that spared not his own Son, but delivered him up for us all, how shall he not with him also freely give you all things?"[2]

But if not,—if the heart, interrogated sincerely, gives an unwilling and unwelcome reply; if there is the love of self there, but not the love of God; if there is the love of the world there, "the lust of the flesh, and the lust of the eyes, and the pride of life," and therefore not the love of God;[3] if religion is a weariness, prayer distasteful, the means of grace neglected; if there are sins committed openly or indulged in secret; if there are bad habits acquiesced in contentedly, or opposed faintly and with scarcely the wish for success; if, in a word, there is the prevalence of the carnal mind,—what shall we say? Certainly, that you have no evidence that you are "the called according to God's purpose;" that you are under condemnation, and in a state of extreme

[1] Rom. viii. 16, 17.   [2] Rom. viii. 32.   [3] 1 John, ii. 15, 16.

danger. But as certainly, that the present is yours to repent and seek salvation; that the offers and promises of God are made to you; that now He is waiting to be gracious. We cannot read the future. Your final destiny, inscribed in the page of God's foreknowledge, is visible to Him alone. But these words we *can* read in the infallible oracles of revealed truth:—" God so loved the world, that he gave his only-begotten Son, that whosoever believeth in him should not perish, but have everlasting life." [1] " God our Saviour would have all men to be saved, and to come unto the knowledge of the truth." [2] " Believe in the Lord Jesus Christ, and thou shalt be saved." [3] " When the wicked man turneth away from his wickedness that he hath committed, and doeth that which is lawful and right, he shall save his soul alive. For I have no pleasure in the death of him that dieth, saith the Lord God: wherefore turn yourselves and live ye." [4] Act upon these promises. Throw yourselves on God's mercy through Christ. Examine your past lives; probe deeply, faithfully, your soul's state. Spread before God the sad discovery of sins committed, and duties neglected, and promises broken; and earnestly ask His forgiveness for His sake who bore those sins upon the cross. And resolve sincerely now, though in distrust of your own strength and in reliance only on His grace, to

[1] John, iii. 16.
[2] 1 Tim. ii. 3, 4.
[3] Acts, xvi. 31.
[4] Ezek. xviii. 27, 32.

live henceforth *religiously*,—as those who are not their own but are bought with a price, as those who are dead to sin and have risen again to righteousness, as those who are strangers here and look for a home in heaven.

And if you find,—as undoubtedly you will,—that your repentance is too cold, and your faith weak, and your falls frequent, and that the flame of love burns dimly where the world has reigned so long; remember for your comfort that the Almighty Spirit is promised to us all; that all that seek shall find; that more readily than earthly parents give good gifts unto their children, your heavenly Father will give the Holy Spirit to them that ask Him. Persevere then; watch and pray. Use with faith and diligence all the means of grace. Wait on the Lord, and serve Him to the utmost of your power, while you wait. Do this in simple trust on Jesus Christ; and I dare pronounce you,—for I rest upon the faithfulness of God,—among those "who are the called according to His purpose," those to whom "all things work together for good."

This privilege of God's people I now proceed to consider,—a topic of consolation and hope to those who love Him; a motive, surely, to return to Him to those who have not loved Him yet. "We know that all things work together for good to them that love God."

1. The words appear, indeed, at variance with facts.

God's servants are not, perhaps, more prosperous than others. Sometimes they seem marked out for calamity, and bowed down by accumulated trials. It is so. But these very afflictions work together for their good. To others, indeed, sorrow and suffering are sometimes made the means of bringing them to God, and by a rough schooling teaching them to love Him. But if they fail in this, they are to them unmixed and unmitigated evil. This they can never be to those who love God. Affliction to them is the chastening of a loving parent, correcting them " for their profit, that they may be partakers of His holiness."[1] It realises to them the precious truth, that their home is not here, but in a region where sorrow and change are not. It aids to wean them from this world and to set their affection on things above. It trains them in habits of patience and submission to their Father's will,—essential features of the Christian's character. It enables them (which else they could not do) to follow the example of their suffering Saviour, that " if so be they suffer with him, they may be also glorified together."[2] It brings with it a happy assurance of their Father's love; "for whom the Lord loveth he chasteneth, and scourgeth every son whom he receiveth."[3] Nay, bitter as it is in itself, it is even the parent of peace and hope and joy. "Not only so," said one who knew its power well, " but we glory in tribulation also: knowing

[1] Heb. xii. 10.   [2] Rom. viii. 17.   [3] Heb. xii. 6.

that tribulation worketh patience; and patience, experience; and experience, hope; and hope maketh not ashamed." [1]

2. There is really more difficulty (though there may seem less) in the belief that prosperity works for the good of those who love God. We have at least as much need to pray for deliverance in all time of our wealth, as in all time of our tribulation. Then the power of the world is greatest. Then the passions have freer range, and the appetites greater excitements. Then God and heaven and the soul's eternal destiny are thrown into the shade by the glitter of things around us. Then selfishness is apt to establish and fortify itself in the breast; and those fearful habits to strengthen,—hardness of heart and contempt of God's word and commandments. But they who love God have a talisman against these dangers. They cannot love Him and the world too: for "if any man love the world, the love of the Father is not in him." [2] Living, then, above the world, though in the world, they enjoy the blessings of prosperity without suffering from its perils. It even enhances their love, by giving them daily fresh cause for gratitude, and lifting their hearts daily in many an aspiration of thankfulness to God. It multiplies their means of doing good; enabling them to employ their wealth, their influence or their example to promote God's glory or their brethren's

[1] Rom. v. 3—5.   [2] 1 John, ii. 15.

good. They may "make themselves friends of the mammon of unrighteousness, that when they fail they may receive them into everlasting habitations."[1] They may employ their health and leisure in works of charity. They may encourage religion and discourage sin. They may "let their light so shine before men, that they may see their good works and glorify their Father which is in heaven."[2]

3. Thirdly, opposition and persecution work together for their good. It is wonderful thus to see God not merely thwarting the designs of His enemies, but using them for His purpose, and making them a blessing to those they hate. It is not only that persecution rooted the tender plant of Christianity, and "the blood of the martyrs was the seed of the Church;" but it carries with it personal benefits to every true Christian. It is the test of their sincerity, "that the trial of their faith, being much more precious than of gold that perisheth, though it be tried with fire, may be found unto praise and honour and glory at the appearing of Jesus Christ."[3] It furnishes a fair field for the exercise of patience, long-suffering, and Christian forgiveness. It brings with it that sweet conviction of God's supporting love, which is never so strongly felt as when all else opposes or forsakes us. It has a great recompense of reward; for "blessed are ye," said our Saviour, "when men shall revile you, and persecute you, and shall say all manner of evil against you falsely for my

[1] Luke, xvi. 9.   [2] Matt. v. 16.   [3] 1 Pet. i. 7.

sake. Rejoice and be exceeding glad: for great is your reward in heaven."[1]

4. But not only the opposition of men,—the enmity of Satan also is overruled for good to those who love God. Temptation, dangerous as it is and, as much as may be, to be avoided, is not without its uses. It is the foe with which the Christian warrior, in the strength of God's grace, must combat for the crown. It is the way in which Christ trod, and we must follow Him. It is the hour of trial in which we learn our own weakness and God's protecting might, and thus are taught at once humility and faith. It is the instrument of our probation; and though to many the occasion of eternal ruin, it is the necessary trial of those who are "the called according to God's purpose." "Blessed is the man that endureth temptation: for when he is tried, he shall receive the crown of life, which the Lord hath promised to them that love him."[2]

5. Nay, even falls into sin,—perilous as they are, disgraceful as they are, painful as they are, beyond any pain this world can inflict,—may yet be made to work for good to those whose hearts are, in the main, with God, and who are deeply grieved at thus offending Him. Their knowledge of their own weakness is increased, and they are led to trust more entirely to God and less to themselves. Their sense of His mercy is heightened, who permits them, stained and humbled as they are, yet to return to Him and find forgiveness

[1] Matt. v. 10, 11.   [2] James, i. 12.

through their Redeemer's blood. Their watchfulness is quickened, both against temptation and over their own hearts, lest they should again be surprised and betrayed. And they use more earnestly the means of grace,—praying, and reading, and hearing, and meditating, and communicating,—that being one with Christ and abiding in Him, they may receive the fulness of His grace and be protected from the evil one.

6. Thus do all things in this life work together for good to them that love God. And that which crowns and consummates their blessings, is that which to human nature is awful, and to the wicked is terror,—death. It is not, indeed, that they are free from that instinctive shrinking from dissolution which is implanted in us for our preservation, or that they can part, though it be but for a time, without some sorrow from those they leave behind. But notwithstanding its solemnity and its separation, to those who love God,—to those to whom "to live is Christ,—to die is gain."[1] It is the passage from sin and imperfection to perfect purity and holiness; from pain and weariness and grief to joy and light and glory; from danger to safety, from earth to heaven, from men to God. It is the hour of faith's accomplishment, when hope melts into fruition. It joins the redeemed to their Saviour, and satisfies the longings of those who have loved their Lord. Painful it may be and awful; many a tie may it break which cannot be sundered

[1] Phil. i. 21.

without a pang; there may be a natural shrinking which even faith cannot altogether check; but those who love God, rejoice to know that it is working for their good; that their pilgrimage is over, their victory won; that they are about "to depart and to be with Christ, which is far better." [1]

And why is this? What is the powerful charm which thus makes all things work together for good to them that love God, and transmutes even evils into a blessing? It is God's love for them. Their love itself wells from this deep source. "We love Him because He first loved us." [2] And what good thing can be wanting to those whom God loves? "He that spared not his own Son but delivered Him up for us all, how shall He not with Him also freely give us all things? Who shall separate us from the love of Christ? shall tribulation, or distress, or persecution, or famine, or nakedness, or peril, or sword? Nay, in all these things we are more than conquerors through Him that loved us. For I am persuaded," adds the Apostle, (and oh, dear brethren, let us pray earnestly that the same happy persuasion may be the comfort of our spirit and the encouragement of our efforts) —"that neither death, nor life, nor angels, nor principalities, nor powers, nor things present, nor things to come, nor height, nor depth, nor any other creature, shall be able to separate us from the love of God, which is in Christ Jesus our Lord."

[1] Phil. i. 23. [2] 1 John, iv. 19.

SERMON IV.

FAITH A GIFT OF THE SPIRIT.

1 Cor. xii. pt. 3.

No man can say that Jesus is the Lord, but by the Holy Ghost.

Perhaps there is no one habit, which Scripture attributes more often, either explicitly or implicitly, to the agency of the Holy Spirit, than a sound and lively faith; and there is none, therefore, which the soul, anxious to find within itself that only credible mark of its justification and predestination to life,— the indwelling of the Spirit,—will more carefully seek and cherish. "No man can come to me," said our Saviour, "except the Father which hath sent me, draw him."[1] And again: "When He, the Spirit of truth is come, He will guide you into all truth . . . . He shall glorify me: for He shall receive of mine, and shall show it unto you."[2] It is in accordance with this declaration that St. Paul wrote, "The natural man receiveth not the things of the Spirit of God: for they are foolishness unto him: neither can he know them, because they are spiritually dis-

---

[1] John, vi. 44.   [2] John, xvi. 13, 14.

cerned."[1] "The Lord," we are told, "opened the heart of Lydia, that she attended unto the things which were spoken of Paul."[2] The Apostle makes the illumination of the heart by the truth of the Gospel a fact analogous to the first illumination of our globe, —a creation, that is, of divine power. "For God, who commanded the light to shine out of darkness, hath shined in our hearts, to give the light of the knowledge of the glory of God in the face of Jesus Christ."[3] And in the words of the text he expressly attributes to the Holy Spirit the belief and confession of the truth. "Now concerning spiritual gifts, brethren, I would not have you ignorant. Ye know that ye were Gentiles, carried away unto these dumb idols, even as ye were led. Wherefore I give you to understand, that no man speaking by the Spirit of God calleth Jesus accursed: and that no man can say that Jesus is the Lord, but by the Holy Ghost." Nay, St. John seems even to propose soundness of faith,—and, that, too, on what men call merely speculative truths,—as the test by which to discern the presence of the Spirit of God from imposture, self-deceit, or the agency of evil spirits. "Beloved, believe not every spirit, but try the spirits whether they are of God: because many false prophets are gone out into the world. Hereby know ye the Spirit of God: Every spirit that confesseth that Jesus Christ is come in the flesh is of God: and every spirit

[1] 1 Cor. iii. 14.   [2] Acts, xvi. 14.   [3] 2 Cor. iv. 6.

that confesseth not that Jesus Christ is come in the flesh is not of God: and this is that spirit of antichrist, whereof ye have heard that it should come, and even now already is it in the world."[1]

But though the doctrine, that faith is the work of the Spirit, is undoubtedly that of Scripture, yet it cannot be denied, that it opens many difficulties, as well as leads to many important practical results.

Faith, in the sense in which we are here concerned with it, is the belief of a professed revelation of God to man on the authority of God who made it; and a *lively* faith is such a conviction of its truth, as causes it to operate as a motive on our affections and lives. It is itself, then, a habit of the intellect, and appears, so far, to become moral only at the point where it influences, rather than is influenced by, the will:—when the judgment, that is, being thoroughly persuaded by the weight of proof, offers to the affections such and such things as realities to be loved or hated, and to the conscience such and such things as duties to be performed or sins to be avoided. And in this light, as a moral motive, coupled too, as it often is in Scripture, with those effects which it should produce on the will, there seems no greater difficulty in viewing faith as a work of the Spirit, than in so regarding repentance, love, or obedience. But in the prior intellectual process,—the conviction of the understanding by the force of proof,—there is a

[1] 1 John, iv. 1—3.

difficulty which has been felt, probably, by most minds. It seems generally to be taken for granted, (and perhaps rightly), that it is in the moral energies of man, and not in his purely intellectual operations, that the influence of the Holy Spirit has place,—in the determination of the will, the scope and intensity of the affections, the character of his ends; and not in the truth of his generalizations or the correctness of his deductions. And although there is no *à priori* objection to the belief, that He who made the mind and distributes its powers in various measure and kind to each even as He will, may interfere directly even in its purely intellectual processes, strengthening the grasp, or clearing the vision, or guiding it along the track of truth; yet it seems more consonant with experience to suppose, that the laws of mind, like those of matter, are usually left by Him who ordained them, to work out their operations without immediate supernatural control. There appears (as far as can be seen) no more reason to seek or expect divine interposition to correct or prevent a logical error, than to stay the effects of any physical power which we ourselves have set in motion. Either would be a miracle, which God *may* work; but which we have no authority to suppose He will.

But if so, in what sense can a sound faith be a work of the Holy Spirit? If we may admit that the motive effects of a truth vividly conceived are brought to bear by His aid upon the affections and the conscience, yet

Faith a Gift of the Spirit. 61

what part can divine grace have had in the previous process, which led the mind to admit and embrace that truth? It seems to be a law of the intellect, that belief necessarily follows the preponderance of apprehended proof, as the scale falls in which the weight is greatest. We can no more refuse to believe what is proved, or believe what is destitute of apparent proof, than the eye can reject or change the forms and colours thrown by external objects on the retina. How then can the reception of a doctrine by the reason be affected by the operations of divine grace? If it is proved, must it not be believed? If it is not proved, must it not be doubted or rejected?

This difficulty however, such as it is, is not peculiar to Scripture, or religious truth, or the question of the Holy Spirit's influence. It belongs equally to the acknowledged fact, that on almost every subject, men, apparently of equivalent power of intellect, with precisely the same evidence before them, arrive at widely different conclusions. Thus it is every day in history, in politics, in much that is called science, in the judgment we form of each other's characters and conduct, and even in the credit that is given to alleged events almost within the sphere of our own observation. True, then, though it may be as a law of the intellect, that belief necessarily follows the preponderance of apprehended proof, it is clear that there must be some other element, which in some way modifies extensively its practical application, and gives room for moral influences, and consequently (if God so will) for the ordinary operations of divine grace, to aid materially in moulding opinion and actuating faith.

It is unnecessary here to draw the distinction between the demonstrations of pure reasoning and moral certainty, which is only a high degree of probability, and which implies at least the possibility of presumptions, however weak, on the other side. But it is important to bear in mind, that in the former case alone is the apprehension of a truth an operation of pure intellect. There, where each step is but the rigorously accurate expansion of a truth embedded in the very texture of the mind, and where the idea of probability has no place, the mental process of apprehending the proof and accepting the conclusion takes effect without any hindrance or interference, excepting such as may be interposed by intellectual weakness or inability for continuous thought. As soon as comprehended, the argument, if sound, is necessarily and irresistibly admitted : the premises were axioms or iron-bound demonstrations, which the feelings have neither the will nor the power to bend ; and of the same character will be the conclusion.

But step off the ground of pure reasoning ; let the subject-matter admit ever so low a degree of contingency ; and the case is changed. Belief, indeed, must still follow acknowledged preponderance of proof ; but in the arrangement and weighing of proof,—now no longer demonstration, but the balance of presumptions,—not intellect merely, but, indirectly at least, the affections and passions, the whole moral constitution, are brought into play. There is nothing so certain which may not admit of a presumption on the other side. You cannot demonstrate that the sun will rise to-morrow; and you might urge in vain the induction of six thousand years against one who was anticipating the contrary from the adoption of some interpretation of prophecy, or even from the impression of some vivid dream. And such presumptions, seized upon by passion or prejudice, magnified by hope or fear, and combined by the ingenuity of a mind unconsciously trying to deceive itself, so modify and complicate the premises with which reason has to work, that it becomes not only possible, but common, for minds of equal power, with precisely the same facts before them, to arrive at very different conclusions. It is not only where the rival schools of some infant science are conflicting with the half-truths of an imperfect induction, that party spirit is suffered to throw its weapon into the rising scale, and the honour of nominalism or realism, of the Vulcanian or the Neptunian theory, to go far to accredit facts without examination, or to give weight to reasoning which does not prove: but even where truth itself is at the end of the investigation, prejudice has often warped the rule of judgment and dimmed the eye of the inquirer. *Facts* have been rejected from the hands of a political opponent; and Newton's discoveries have been impugned, because made by an Englishman.

It is evidently not incumbent on the theologian, however interesting it may be to the moral philosopher, to analyse the operation, by which, in all cases where the contingency of the subject-matter renders presumptions on either side possible, moral agency may step in to modify, not indeed the bare reasoning process itself, but the antecedents and materials (as it were) of that process, so as to affect the conclusion drawn, and consequently the whole circle of opinion and belief.

Whether it be, that a partial and temporary blindness of the judgment is superinduced by the force of passion and the tension of the will; or whether (as seems more probable) *attention*, the optic glass, or rather the eye of the mind, is directed by the prevailing emotion excited by the subject in question, with more intensity on a certain class of considerations bearing upon it, while others it glances over slightly, or entirely disregards—(even as the bodily eye gazing fixedly on one object, is as blind for the time to all the rest as if they were not)—so that from all the topics which should have been considered in due weight and measure, it culls those only which lead to the desired conclusion, or gives them such undue prominence in the field of vision, that the judgment, deceived and misled, arrives at a partial, though acceptable, decision: these are questions which may be left to the metaphysician to solve. It is enough for us, that the fact is admitted, that everywhere, but in the necessary truths of demonstrative reasoning, the conclusions of reason are actually modified by the wishes, interests, or prejudices of the reasoner; so that belief is not merely the result of intellect, but is, in perhaps a large majority of cases, the mixed product of the moral and intellectual faculties combined.

And if this be true where the feelings and passions are only remotely affected, and should not be so at all; how much more will it have place, when the subject-matter is religion; which must touch the tenderest parts of our moral nature; which strikes on hopes and fears which vibrate through eternity; which bears directly on every affection, passion, motive, habit, and act; which, if admitted to be true, requires a complete revolution in the whole inner man, and in great part of the outward conduct. It is obvious how many disturbing influences must be set at work, when the truth or falsehood of such claims and obligations is in question; how many hopes, and fears, and desires; how great a mist of prejudice, distorting some facts, magnifying others, concealing others; what a phantasmagoria of objections, bright with the borrowed colours of the feelings, and refracted to undue magnitude by the wishes of the heart: and this both when the question is formally examined by a mind consciously and continuously seeking the truth; and still more so when,

F

as by most men, it is solved almost unconsciously, and by fragmentary processes, and the edifice of their faith is built up gradually by little additions of conviction, or sapped by degrees by objections caught up here and there, as it were by hazard, and welcomed and assimilated by a willing mind. The choice or arrangement of the materials with which reason is to work, is much in the power of the will; and the will is prejudiced, and cannot, or will not, honestly do its part.

It is not, then, surprising, that our Lord should have attributed unbelief always to moral, never to purely intellectual causes. "He that believeth on the Son of God is not condemned: but he that believeth not is condemned already, because he hath not believed in the name of the only-begotten Son of God. And this is the condemnation, that light is come into the world, and men loved darkness rather than light, because their deeds were evil. For every one that doeth evil hateth the light, neither cometh to the light, lest his deeds should be reproved."[1] "Ye will not (οὐ θέλετε) come to me that ye might have life . . . How can ye believe, which receive honour one of another, and seek not the honour which cometh from God only?"[2] While on the other hand he declares, "If any man will (ἐάν τις θέλῃ) do his will, he shall know of the doctrine whether it be of God, or whether I speak of myself."[3]

[1] John, iii. 18—20.   [2] John, v. 40, 44.
[3] John, vii. 17.

It will follow too,—which is the point more immediately before us,—not only that in the formation of a sound and living faith there is room for the agency of the Holy Spirit, but that without His aid such faith cannot exist. For if the character of our belief depends not merely on the correctness of the reasoning process, but much more on prior operations of the will, by which the antecedents and materials of reasoning are selected and arranged; and if our moral nature is in our unregenerate state warped and impaired, so as to have a disinclination to what is good and a bias to what is evil; it is evident that the Gospel, placed before such a tribunal, must be tried by a prejudiced and incapable judge; that, being wished false, and admitting of objections capable of being magnified and coloured into refutations, it is certain to be found false; and that nothing can rectify the balance of judgment, and place truth on an equal footing with falsehood, but the same external and divine power which changes and renews the will of man, and enables it to love right instead of wrong, and to desire in all things to know and do God's will. And thus we arrive at the truth contained in our Lord's declaration, " No man can come unto me, except the Father which hath sent me draw him;" and cannot but admit the strict accuracy of the expression in the inspired narrative of St. Luke; " whose heart the Lord opened, that she attended unto the things which were spoken of Paul."

In a similar way it may be inferred that belief, not only in Christianity in general as a revelation from God, but in each of the main doctrines of Christianity, is the work of the Spirit; so that "no man can say that Jesus is the Lord but by the Holy Ghost," and "every spirit that confesseth that Jesus Christ is come in the flesh is of God." Each doctrine, being practical and involving certain duties, acts upon the moral choice; and accordingly as this is warped by natural pravity, or rectified by divine grace, the presumptions for and against the doctrine may be partially or impartially considered, and the conclusion may be error, or truth.

But this is a subject which we cannot follow up at present: it must be sufficient to have indicated the line, on which moral philosophy coincides with the declarations of Scripture. Let us now, in further illustration of what has been said, endeavour to trace in one or two instances the process by which moral causes, acting on the intellect, may lead to avowed or practical unbelief.

1. In a certain class of minds infidelity and heresy alike seem to owe their origin to intellectual pride. Conscious of mental power, eager to display it by originality of thought, impatient even of *appearing* to follow without inquiry in the track marked out by others, they are (till disciplined by divine grace) singularly ill-prepared for the reception of religious truth. In this there is no scope for daring hypothesis

or the bold flight of discovery. Its truths are true, on the very condition of being old. It is a revelation from God to man; and was as complete when first made, as it is now or ever will be. Defended it may be; defined it may be; explained it may be; but it cannot be altered, without ceasing to be truth. To develope, (meaning, to add), is as unlawful as to detract. To believe, therefore, is to adopt the same opinions which have been the creed of multitudes before, and to be confounded in the mass of unreasoning minds which have received implicitly the same traditionary tenets. Objections, on the other hand, have an air of novelty. There is at least the appearance of power in striking out difficulties. It implies strength to swim against the current of traditionary prejudices and the settled conviction of ages. It is an intoxicating pleasure to feel different from other men, (that is, in our own judgment, superior to them), and the brain often reels under it.

Besides this, there is a prejudice against the Gospel from the mere circumstance of its being old. In every science new discoveries are making daily. The landmarks of knowledge are perpetually being moved forward. Acknowledged facts are shown to be vulgar errors; and popular belief has ceased to be a guarantee, or even a presumption, of truth. Hence, by a natural fallacy, the antiquity of an opinion itself suggests a doubt. In history, in politics, in science, men have long been mistaken; why not in religion also?

With such feelings and prepossessions the mind catches up objections to Christianity, or to some of its doctrines, as just what it was expecting to find. It dwells on them: it magnifies them by the exclusion of other presumptions, till they fill the field of the mental vision, and leave no room for truth. Arguments on the other side are slightly examined and gladly dismissed; and especially if (as must often be the case) they do not so much solve satisfactorily the difficulties which occupy the mind, as endeavour to outbalance them by the weight of evidence, and by the counter-difficulties which attend on unbelief. A favourite objection will not be thus dislodged. It has a powerful ally in the pride which wishes to maintain it. And thus we too often see the spectacle of men of strong intellect, acute thinkers, eminent, perhaps, in literature and science, becoming infidels, sceptics, or heretics,—not because there is not sufficient evidence of truth; not because they had it not before them; but because they began with a prepossession for error; because intellectual pride had secretly prejudiced their decision; and the perverted will had shackled the free processes of reason. "How can ye believe," said our Lord, "which receive honour one of another, and seek not the honour that cometh from God only?" Humility and faith are kindred gifts of the same Spirit.

2. Another source of unbelief is even more evidently moral. It arises when the soul would hide

from God, after displeasing Him by wilful sin. I will take the case of those who have been trained to know God. Having been baptized into His Church, they have been taught as they were able to learn,—" line upon line, and precept upon precept,"—what He has done for them, and what they have promised to do for Him. They have been made acquainted with His dealings with mankind, and with His unspeakable love in the redemption of the world by Jesus Christ. They have been early accustomed to draw near to Him in prayer; and conscience has at once directed their thoughts to Him, as they did well or ill. And they should have gone on, cherishing the spark of grace by watchfulness and self-control and the use of all the appointed means, growing in holiness, and drawing daily nearer to God.

But temptation under some form or another came,—temptation to some *known* sin: not without plausible excuses indeed,—(for when did Satan ever want a veil to throw over sin's deformity?)—but still excuses which never really satisfied their better mind. They parleyed with it, hesitated, yielded, and sinned. Immediately their eyes were opened. They knew that they were fallen; that they had offended God. The peace of their bosom was gone. They were restless and dissatisfied with self; and a cloud, as it were, had settled between their souls and the light of God's countenance. They were ashamed to come before Him. And here is the fatal step. Had they forced themselves to "arise and go to their Father, and say unto him, Father, I have sinned against heaven and before thee, and am no more worthy to be called thy son:"[1] had they sought His pardon at once in unreserved confession, sorrowful repentance, and earnest prayer; He would have "hidden his face from their sins, and blotted out all their iniquities;" would have "restored unto them the joy of His salvation, and upheld them with His free Spirit."[2] But it was not so. They wanted honest courage to probe the shame and guilt; or they secretly loved the sin, even while they writhed under the sting of conscience; or the proud heart would not bend to the humiliation of confession and penitence; or to retrace their steps would interfere with their worldly prospects, or subject them to ridicule, and the reproach of men. They tried to hide from God. They drowned, as best they might, the whispers of His Spirit. They shrank from thinking of Him. Communion with Him in prayer was neglected, or gladly omitted on any excuse, or became a mere form of words without the heart, pressed down by an incubus against which they did not care to struggle.

This is a painful state; and men will not rest long in it without seeking an anodyne. Some, for example, smother accusing thoughts in worldly amusements and the dissipation of frivolous gaiety. Uneasy in themselves, they involve themselves in a whirl of

---

[1] Luke, xv. 21. [2] Ps. li. 9, 12.

pleasures which take them out of self. And doubtless they succeed. The mind cannot be filled with two objects at once. But what a wretched success! to cheat the perishing soul with a false security, which will probably desert it, just when it is most needed, in sickness, sorrow, and the death-bed, and will assuredly fail it at the judgment day.

But many,—far more, probably, than can be known till the secrets of all hearts are disclosed,—take refuge in a kind of partial unbelief. There are difficulties in revelation, and in some of its doctrines,—light as a feather, indeed, when weighed impartially in the balance against the accumulated evidences of truth, but not, of course, without weight when poised and pondered over by themselves. Such the writhing soul is glad to seize. He wishes to escape from God: —at any rate from the God of the Gospel, the God of his baptism. Suppose the Gospel should not be true, his obligations are imaginary, and his guilt and ingratitude are unreal. He almost wishes it were so. In this state he imbibes readily some one or more of the objections to Christianity which have never wanted agents to disseminate them, and which are supplied abundantly in the popular literature of the day, hinted in an allusion, or suggested by a sneer. The poison works. He does not, perhaps, follow up the train of thought thus opened, nor trace the tortuous mazes of *reasoning* infidelity. He has found enough to satisfy him for the present. The Gospel *may not* be true. He may not be the ungrateful and inexcusable offender against a God of love, which conscience has told him he is. There may not be the stern eye of a Father's displeasure fixed upon him. There may be no judgment to come: all may be well hereafter. Reason is soon satisfied, where the feelings are already engaged. Though not, perhaps, confessing infidelity even to himself, he accepts the doubts he feels and cherishes, as an answer to the accusations and an excuse to the demands of conscience. Why should he be disquieted about what, after all, may not be true? Meanwhile his outward life is perhaps little changed. He remains upright in his dealings with men, respected even and beloved. He may not even omit the forms of religious duty: nay, (mysterious as it is) he may be the instrument of leading others to righteousness. But the jewel is gone from the casket: the *soul* of religion is dead.

There are many and weighty reasons, brethren, why the Christian should be watchful and anxious indeed not to grieve the Spirit, and dim by sin the light that is in him. Let the considerations on which we have been dwelling, add one more earnest warning to vigilance and self-control. On a conscience void of offence and the consequent continued presence of the Spirit may depend the faith on which depends eternity. Every admitted sin, every passion indulged, every selfish habit gratified, every vain thought encouraged or unchecked, is not only leaving its stain upon the soul, to be washed off (if washed off at all) only by the blood of the Lamb from the sincerely penitent; but it is sapping the foundations of a sound belief; strengthening the prejudices and feelings which warp the moral judgment; dimming the eye of reason; and preparing, gradually it may be, but surely, what the Apostle calls, "the evil heart of unbelief." As the light of the Spirit is withdrawn, the shadows of doubt and error darken. Scared by difficulties of its own seeking, or following reasons it wished to find sufficient, the mind, misled by sin or over-balanced by presumption, runs into some deadly heresy, or settles into fatal unbelief. Not to Timothy merely; not to ministers of the Gospel only; but to each of us, according to the grace given us, should the Apostle's words have a warning voice: "This charge I commit unto thee according to the prophecies which went before on thee, that thou by them mightest war a good warfare; holding faith and a good conscience, which some having put away, concerning faith have made shipwreck." [1]

[1] 1 Tim. i. 18, 19.

SERMON V.

FAITH A GIFT OF THE SPIRIT.

ACTS, xv. 8, 9.

And God, which knoweth the hearts, bare them witness, giving them the Holy Ghost, even as he did unto us; and put no difference between us and them, purifying their hearts by faith.

THE faith which is the work of the Holy Spirit, and which must therefore be consulted by the soul as an element in the reply to be made by herself to that solemn question, Have I the Spirit of God? must possess two qualities. It must be sound, and it must be practical. The Holy Ghost is not the author of error; nor, on the other hand, can His energy be inferred from the mere assent given by the understanding to speculative truth. It has, indeed, been denied, that moral influences have any effect on the conclusions of reason and the formation of opinion; and consequently, as the Holy Spirit, as far as we are taught, acts only morally,—on the affections and will, not on· the reason and judgment,—it is held that belief, as far as it is the apprehension of truth and assent given to doctrines, lies without the circle of His ordinary operations. We have seen, however, on a former occasion, that, in point of fact, the process of believing *is* affected extensively by moral influences; and that, too, not merely in religion, and in other subjects which touch most closely the passions, affections, and prejudices, but also in matters which, one would think, are or ought to be, indifferent ; and we found, that, though the will may not invalidate the purely logical operation of drawing the conclusion from the premises, yet in the formation of those premises,—in selecting and grouping the evidence, in throwing a partial light on the presumptions for or against the truth, and in directing the attention to the arguments or objections on the one side rather than to those on the other,—the feelings and wishes of the heart have very great power over the results of reasoning, which in fact they usually modify, and often mould. It follows, therefore, that the Holy Spirit, even though working merely on the moral part of our constitution and influencing the affections and the will, may be the main agent in determining and forming our belief; and Scripture repeatedly testifies that He is. It will follow too, that, as the Spirit of truth cannot be the Author of anything but truth, so a sound faith alone can be recognised as His work. And, therefore, as "no man can say that Jesus is the Lord, but by the Holy Ghost, so no man speaking by the Spirit of God calleth Jesus accursed,"[1] and " every spirit that con-

[1] 1 Cor. xii. 3.

fesseth not that Jesus Christ is come in the flesh, is not of God."[1]

It is not necessary, however, to conclude, that the presence of the Spirit is incompatible with every error, even in spiritual things, or that he who is led by the Spirit of God, is in every respect infallible. This conclusion would well-nigh close the kingdom of heaven, and would render the seal of the Spirit almost impossible to be recognised. It was the promise, indeed, made to the Apostles, that "when he, the Spirit of truth was come, he would guide them into all truth,"—the whole truth;[2] a promise, which in their case was necessary, not for the salvation of their own souls, but to the infallibility of that universal rule of faith which was to be embodied from their inspired teaching, secured in written documents, and handed down together with the canon of the Old Testament, as the only faultless standard of truth and falsehood, even to the consummation of all things. But to other Christians, to whose errors no such consequences attach, grace is doubtless given to establish them in all truth necessary for their salvation; and this is the work of the Holy Ghost: but if there be revealed verities, as doubtless there are, which we may mistake or be ignorant of, and yet be saved, it must not be inferred that where these are not, there cannot be the presence of the Spirit, "who divideth to every man severally as he will."[3] And

[1] John, iv. 3. [2] Εἰς πᾶσαν τὴν ἀλήθειαν. John, xvi. 13.
[3] 2 Cor. xii. 11.

Faith a Gift of the Spirit.

even as in the renovation of the moral character, "the infection of nature doth remain, yea in them that are regenerate," and many a foible and fault mars the holiness of God's own saints, and the inward struggle which attests the life of sin in the members, is so far from being a proof of the absence of the Spirit, that it may rather be the token that His energy is striving there;—so it is very possible for the main truths of the Gospel to be grasped and held fast in His strength, and the soul's salvation to be anchored on the rock, even though some errors may be held in the same embrace, and we may yet be tossed on some unquiet wave of doubt. The foundation may be rightly laid, though "wood, hay, stubble," may as yet be built upon it.

This remark may be necessary for the comfort of those, who, while they have received with a living faith the promises of God in Jesus Christ, and are endeavouring to adorn the doctrine of God their Saviour in all things, are yet harassed with difficulties and doubts in minor points (which however assume an importance precisely because they harass), and are tempted to question the presence of the informing Spirit, as if they were reprobates; or to long for some external infallible authority on which to throw themselves and be at rest, and, therefore, to "believe the lie" of that Church, which professes to be, what God has never given, an unerring interpreter of His revealed word. The *love* of truth, God's truth, where-ever it may be found, is an indispensable criterion of the teaching of the Spirit; but the possession and enjoyment of *all* truth, is not.

And it is also important to bear this distinction in mind, when we judge of others. There are, indeed, broad truths involving salvation, and marked out as such in Scripture, the denial of which is not compatible with the Spirit of Christ; and there are errors, therefore, the holders of which we are to " save with fear, pulling them out of the fire,"[1] and to the teachers of which we may not "bid God speed."[2] But where other minor errors are held in the meekness of a holy life; where the fruits of the Spirit are undeniably manifest, though the tares of some mistaken doctrine may be among them; who are we that we should deny the presence in such weak brethren of the spirit of holiness, or reject them as members of that invisible body of Christ, the parts of which are knit together by the one invisible Spirit? If they are led by the Spirit of God, they are the sons of God; and we may not banish them from His family. We cannot, perhaps, worship with them on earth: we may yet hope to hold happy communion with them in heaven.

We might now pass on from the consideration of *soundness* of faith as an essential feature in the witness of the Spirit, but that one or two practical consequences lie on the surface, which it will be neces-

[1] Jude, 23. [2] 2 John, 10.

sary only to indicate. It is, indeed, sufficiently obvious (would that it were sufficiently borne in mind!)—that the first requisite for the attainment of religious truth is an obedient life. "If any man will do His will, he shall know of the doctrine whether it be of God."[1] Not only are the main obstacles removed, which impede the impartial search after truth; not only is that dislike to holiness diminished which makes sensual and selfish men almost long for unbelief; not only are those passions and affections moderated, which, when indulged, throw into such undue prominence every argument and objection against the truth, and the will is brought more into harmony with the tone of the Gospel; but the Holy Spirit, the Teacher and Guide, will not dwell with the unholy. If a sound faith is His work, it must be sought in the habitual submission of the desires and will to the will of God, and in careful abstinence from every sin which grieves the Spirit, and desecrates His temple in the breast. A sensual, self-indulgent life leads either to the belief of error, or to the holding truth without believing it.

But if the grosser sins are more deadly, they are also more patent; and there are other obstacles to a sound faith which we may admit almost unconsciously. There are intellectual sins, so to speak, scarcely less dangerous to the growth of a healthy belief,—pride, vanity, love of eminence, and especially that deceiv-

[1] John, vii. 17.

ing and self-deceiving semblance of humility, which hungers for the praise it seems to shun, and with sunk head and downcast eyes drinks in with greedy ear the faintest whisper of applause. "God resisteth the proud, but giveth grace unto the humble."[1] And therefore it is especially,—because the Holy Spirit does not dwell in the vain, or ambitious breast,—that our Lord asked, "How can ye believe, which receive honour one of another, and seek not the honour that cometh from God only?"[2] And as a life of sensual indulgence leads not seldom to open infidelity or to dull, hard unbelief; so misbelief is the offspring often of that worm in the core of religion, pride shrouding in the garb of devotion and humility. And, therefore, the student of divine truth, while he keeps himself pure from all stains of the world and the flesh, must daily seek the grace of honest humility,—not pretending to be what he is not, nor dissembling what he thinks he is, but learning from God in prayer to know himself, and, in a fervent desire for His approbation "who seeth in secret," to lose all relish for the unreal gratification of merely human praise or admiration.

I need hardly add, that if a sound faith be the work of the Spirit, and not the mere product of study or intellectual power, it should be made the subject of special and earnest prayer. It should form part of our daily petitions, that God would lead us into the

[1] James, iv. 6.   [2] John, v. 44.

whole truth, and keep us in it. It was the continual prayer of Paul for the Churches, the care of which came daily upon him, that their faith and holiness might strengthen and grow together. He writes, for example, to the Colossians, "For this cause, we also, since the day we heard of it, do not cease to pray for you, and to desire that ye might be filled with the knowledge of his will, in all wisdom and spiritual understanding; that ye might walk worthy of the Lord unto all pleasing, being fruitful in every good work, and increasing in the knowledge of God."[1] And the Student in Theology should remember, that study unsanctified by prayer, — fervent, believing prayer,—is but ill calculated to arrive at truth, still less to issue in a living, justifying faith.

For, on the other hand, the faith which is the work, and therefore an evidence of the Spirit, is not only sound in all essential points, but *practical*. I need hardly say, that it is very possible to hold a scheme of doctrine free from error, to have an accurate knowledge of the creed and its meaning, to be able to defend its articles, and to dissect with nice hand the plausible substitutions of heresy, nay, even to have been conscious of no doubt of the truth of what is held, and yet to be without a living faith. Theology may be learnt like any other science. It is embodied in formularies, taught by books and lectures, digested into systems, analysed, and proved in detail. It has

[1] Col. i. 9, 10.

its questions and controversies, which have been, and are, the arena on which the conflicts of intellect take place; and which, therefore, acquire an interest perfectly independent of the practical importance to the soul's welfare of the truths which are the subjects and the prize of the combat. And just in proportion as Christianity is studied *as a science*, rather than as a professed revelation bearing directly on our affections, duties, and destinies, we shall be less exposed, on the one hand, to those disturbing influences, which (as we have seen) arising from the moral constitution, modify and often warp the conclusions of reason, and the resulting scheme of doctrine may be correct and complete; but on the other, we shall be in great danger of remaining contented with a mere intellectual apprehension of truth, holding the Gospel only as one, even though the noblest and purest, of those forms of verities which we have traced through the history of philosophy; substituting knowledge for faith, the symmetrical and finished statue for the less perfect, perhaps, but living and acting body. And the risk is the greater, because theology, scientifically studied, possesses great and engrossing interest, and the mind may be occupied by it, and even the feelings engaged in its controversies,—as they may in history, or philosophy, or any subject where opposition provokes earnestness;—and we may imagine that we are religious, because our thoughts are exercised about religion; that we are zealous for God, because we are

Faith a Gift of the Spirit. 85

zealous in defence of some doctrine of God's revelation; and that we have faith, because we are contending earnestly for the faith. And the warning is especially necessary in the present day, when the unhappy controversies of our times and (may we not venture to hope) some growing earnestness in sacred things have made points of doctrine ordinary topics of conversation among all classes; and men's minds warm with the subject, and their affections are engaged to this or that party, and they are in danger of mistaking their roused feelings for religion.

Let me, then, remind you, that it is very possible not only to be interested in such topics, but even to be a sound theologian, stored with learning and acute in reasoning, and to have done good service to the truth and the Church by standing in the breach and beating off the assault of the enemy, and yet, while perhaps we know it not, to be without *truth in the heart*, the faith which justifies a sinner before God. And we are warned by the sad associations of to-day,[1] that sincere and earnest men may contend for religion with weapons of a very different temper, may zealously do evil in the name of the Lord, and for the faith which worketh by love may substitute unconsciously a knowledge which worketh by hate.

There is the additional peril in the scientific study of theology without a practical reception of its truths, that it familiarizes us with those great motives

[1] Preached on January 30th.

which, in the hands of the Spirit, are intended to repair and recreate the inner man, without changing us by their influence, and, therefore, deprives them for the future of their edge and power. I need not remind you of that law of our nature, by which habits of action are strengthened by repetition, while the force of passive impressions is weakened. But consider how momentous must be its influence on the health of the soul, when the impressions thus gradually effaced, are such as should be imprinted by the contemplation of our sin and God's mercy, of the wonderful scheme of redemption planned and executed by the Triune Godhead, of death and judgment, of heaven and hell, and above all, of the love of Christ which passeth knowledge. To have much in our thoughts these affecting truths, which in the force of their first novelty ought to stir the very depths of our souls, to be examining, proving, analyzing, classifying them, and not to act upon them as the truths by which we live, is to allow a slow but certain palsy to creep over our feelings, and the incrustations of habit so to harden over our hearts, that the motives of the Gospel, sharp though they should be as a two-edged sword, glance off unfelt and almost unnoticed. This is the especial danger of the theologian in his closet and of the minister in his parish, to live among sacred things without being affected by them, till the soul's medicines lose their efficacy by being used so often. While then you search the truth, live up to the truth. Let each doctrine be applied as a motive, and acted on as a principle. Ask in each instance, not only, If this be truth, what does it concern me to know? but What does it oblige me to do? —and on your soul's peril, go and do it. Thus will habit, instead of enervating the religious feelings, perform its divinely appointed work of expanding Christian principles into Christian practice; and the knowledge, which, as a mere scientific acquirement, could only harden and condemn, will become a living power,—faith in the heart,—throbbing in every pulse, and present in every movement of the spiritual man.

And such is the faith which is the fruit and witness of the Spirit. On this point Holy Scripture is perfectly unambiguous. The words of the text alone would suffice to show, that the faith which accompanied the presence of the Holy Ghost, exercised a renewing power on the moral principles and conduct. "And God, which knoweth the hearts," said St. Peter, speaking of the reception of the Gospel by the Gentiles, "bare them witness, giving them the Holy Ghost even as he did unto us; and put no difference between us and them, purifying their hearts by faith." If it is the teaching of one Apostle, that "Faith, if it hath not works, is dead being alone,"[1] so it is as clearly that of another, who yet is foremost in stating and defending the doctrine of justification by faith only, that a loving, and therefore an obedient, faith,

[1] James, ii. 17.

is the only faith which justifies. "For we through the Spirit," he writes, "wait for the hope of righteousness by faith. For in Jesus Christ neither circumcision availeth anything, nor uncircumcision, but faith which worketh by love."[1] And St. John attributes to this principle the Christian's conquest over "the lust of the flesh, the lust of the eyes, and the pride of life." "This is the victory that overcometh the world, even our faith."[2] But the epistle to the Hebrews should place it beyond doubt, that the faith through which sinners are saved, and which is the Spirit's gift, is so firm a conviction of God's revealed word and promises, that we act upon it in obedience to Him. The faith, which is "the substance of things hoped for, the evidence of things not seen," is that by which Abel offered a more acceptable sacrifice, Enoch walked with God, Noah built the ark, Abraham left his own country and offered up his son, Moses chose rather to suffer affliction with the people of God than to enjoy the pleasures of sin for a season, and all God's saints wrought righteousness or endured afflictions, desiring a better country and "that they might obtain a better resurrection."[3]

It is clear, then, that the assent of the reason to the truths of God's revelation is only an element in the faith which is the work of the Spirit. It may, indeed, be a very small element, as in the case of many simple-minded Christians, who believe for no

[1] Gal. v. 5, 6.   [2] 1 John, v. 4.   [3] See Heb. xi.

stronger reason than that they were taught in youth that the Gospel is true, or that they have found it answering to the needs of their soul, the key which unlocked their heart's secret difficulties; but who yet act upon their belief as unhesitatingly and trustingly, as if they had been convinced by a miracle from heaven, or could bind each truth in the knot of insoluble demonstration. It cannot be so with us, brethren. For our own sakes and for the sake of others, we must endeavour to ground our faith on the rational conviction of the understanding; and with prayer for the teaching of the Spirit, and in the obedience of a holy life, we must seek truth with an earnest purpose to find it and hold it fast. And this foundation of a sound and manly belief, this rooting and grounding in faith, when proved to be so by the superstructure and the growth, is a work of God by the Holy Ghost.

But as the possession of a sound scheme of doctrine is not, of itself, a living faith, so neither is trust or affiance on the merits of Jesus Christ. This is, indeed, another element, and a necessary one. For if it is part, and the most prominent part of the revelation made to us in the Gospel, that Jesus Christ has suffered for and instead of us, and is the propitiation for the sins of the whole world, so that all that believe in him shall not perish but have everlasting life, and there is now no condemnation to them which are in Christ Jesus,—not to trust in

His sacrifice and mediation, when we have turned to God with a contrite heart, or to trust in anything else instead of, or together with Him, is, in fact, " not to believe the record that God gave of his Son."[1] It is to doubt what God has said. And even when the doubt arises from humility and a conviction of exceeding sinfulness, so that the soul conceives itself fixed beyond the circle of pardoning love, yet is it unbelief, setting limits to God's mercy or power, which He has not set; and crediting our own fears or our conceptions of what He must do, instead of His promises and assurances of what He will do. And, therefore, where the Holy Spirit works faith, there will be a simple, confiding reliance for pardon, acceptance and glory on the merits and mediation of Jesus Christ, and on these alone; because for his sake they are offered in the Gospel to *all* penitent and believing sinners.

But, then, there may be such a reliance, where there is no faith working by love or purifying the heart, and consequently where there is not the evidence of the Spirit. I stop not to inquire, whether it be from hypocrisy ripened into self-deceit, or by a delusion of the evil one; yet men are found, even on the death-bed, trusting in Christ, yet continuing in sin. And in a less developed form of the error, a vague reliance upon Christ's merits, sufficient to still the fears of conscience, is often co-existent with a self-indulgent,

[1] 1 John, v. 10.

Faith a Gift of the Spirit. 91

worldly, selfish life. This may, indeed, be reduced under the head of unsound faith. It is partial unbelief. There is a conviction that Christ has died for our sins, and that we can be saved only through him; but there is no conviction of the truths revealed with equal certainty, that our moral character must be changed and renewed by the Holy Spirit, that we must be judged according to our works, and that "without holiness no man shall see the Lord." It is, therefore, that usual form of error, imperfect or dislocated truth; and it is precisely the error which is most congenial to the wishes of the unrenewed heart, because it does, what the practical working of the Romish Church effects more systematically in other ways—offers security without requiring holiness, and has an opiate for fear without a cross for sin. But such a reliance, though it borrow the name of faith, is so far from being the work of the Spirit, that it is the natural and rank produce of "the evil heart of unbelief."

True faith, the gift of the Spirit, is so strong a conviction of all the main truths of God's revelation to us, that we act upon them. They are not theorems to be examined, nor propositions to be proved, but principles by which we must live. They are realities to the soul. And even as the material world in which we exist, and the objects which surround us, and our bodily wants, and the impressions on our senses, are at every moment affecting our feelings, and determining our wills, and giving birth to our actions; so do the invisible verities of revelation, when apprehended by a living faith, act habitually upon the affections, and purposes, and choice, and the whole conduct of the true believer. And thus faith lives, or " Christ dwells in the heart by faith," or the Holy Spirit works by faith (which is itself His work) when faith makes truths influence us as realities. Faith trusts in simple reliance on Jesus Christ, because it is convinced that he is the only and all-sufficient propitiation for all the sins of the whole world. Faith " worketh by love," becauses it realizes the affecting conception of God's unspeakable love to man, and " we love him because he first loved us;" and because it, at the same time, assents to the truth of the inference, " If God so loved us, we ought also to love one another."[1] Faith "overcometh the world;" because it is fully persuaded that "if any man love the world the love of the Father is not in him," that this world is not our home but the pilgrimage only towards a better, and that, if we are in earnest to resist its temptations, "greater is he that is in us, than he that is in the world."[2] Faith " purifies the heart;" for it has a felt certainty that sin cannot enter heaven, and that " the pure in heart" alone " shall see God;"[3] because it embraces, claims, and receives His promises of sanctifying grace; and because, having in itself the hope that " when he shall appear we shall be like him, for we shall see him

[1] 1 John, iv. 11. [2] 1 John, iv. 4. [3] Matt. v. 8.

as he is," it leads us to " purify ourselves even as he is pure." [1] In a word, faith " hath works;" because it brings to bear upon us from the pages of Scripture, now felt to be the voice of the living God, every motive which can act on our moral constitution;—duty and interest, hope and fear, gratitude and a constraining love;—and combines them all towards one end, our holiness, which is at the same time God's service, and our soul's safety.

Let it be this faith, then, brethren, which we seek in our studies, our prayers, and our lives. Let us obey that we may believe; and believe that we may be enabled to obey. Let us do our heavenly Father's will, that we may know of the doctrine whether it be of God; and whatever doctrine we find to be of God, let us act upon it at once and unreservedly, as part of His known will. Let the convictions of our understanding and reason have their full influence on our will; and let our faith be known by our works, "as a tree discerned by the fruit." Thus only may we recognise in it a " tree of our heavenly Father's planting." Thus only may we humbly hope that " Christ is in us of a truth." Thus only will the " Spirit bear witness with our Spirit that we are the children of God."

[1] 1 John, iii, 2, 3.

SERMON VI.

GRACE: THE PERSONAL AGENCY OF THE HOLY SPIRIT.

Romans, viii. 14.

As many as are led by the Spirit of God, they are the sons of God.

It has often been remarked, that Holy Scripture does not teach systems of theology. It states doctrines as facts,— God-taught truths,—which it enunciates for the most part, from time to time, as it pursues the course of narrative, or devotional poetry, or epistolary correspondence, without staying to classify, systematize, or even reconcile them. But it is not, perhaps, observed so frequently, how constantly human systems and theories are destroyed by Holy Scripture; and, sound and solid though they appear when viewed by themselves, melt away when the test of the word of God is fairly and honestly applied. It is tacitly assumed, though it could never be proved, that God has revealed, not only so much truth as is necessary for our duty and salvation, but the whole circle of truth respecting spiritual things and the procedures of his moral government: and men, not content with those segments on which the light of revelation shines brightly, apply themselves to fill up the dark intervals which God has left in mystery, with their own deductions or conjectures. And there is great fascination in a well-built theory; and a scheme of doctrine which is compact and consistent, has to most minds a verisimilitude and a strong presumption of truth. But when brought to the test of Scripture, admitted on all hands to be the rule, if not the only rule, of faith, these complete systems will not square with it. It becomes necessary to explain away God's word, or to dislocate the parts and alter the proportions of its teaching, placing detached passages in undue prominence, and lightly passing other portions by: or to bring in a supplemental rule of faith, which being the interpreter of, becomes in fact the substitute for, Scripture. And thus only does the elaborate theory of Romanism stand erect, and throws over many minds the spell of its apparent completeness, not merely unsupported by God's word, but with God's word bearing ceaseless witness against it. And many other systems can be maintained only by the partial abrogation of the authority of Scripture,—the logical compactness, *e.g.* of Calvinism, or the level common sense (as it is thought) of Arminianism. The rule of faith must be twisted, or stretched, or pared away; and a meaning must often be extorted, almost the reverse of what the language would naturally be understood to mean. Use the supremacy of God's word fairly and honestly;

and it will soon discover a weak part, where human reason or imagination have built their own material on the divine foundation.

So it is with all theories of the *mode* in which supernatural influence acts upon and ameliorates man's moral nature. Holy Scripture is distinct in revealing the fact and the necessity of a great moral change which we call sanctification, of which the Holy Spirit is the Agent, and the affections, the judgment, the moral choice, and consequently the life and character of the individual man, is the subject. In the revelation of this fact it employs various figures and analogies, borrowed from processes or relations with which we are familiar, and well adapted to impress the fact on us; but not always consistent with one another. As the truth is to be presented to us in this or that aspect, it is illustrated by different, and not necessarily cognate or even parallel, analogies.

Of the mode in which spiritual influence acts upon a moral agent, Scripture says nothing. It leaves this unrevealed, as it does all other metaphysical problems, the solution of which is not essential to practice. But the terminology it uses, is suggestive of theories. It could hardly be otherwise, being adopted from familiar analogies, in order to convey the truth forcibly to the universal mind of man. Here, then, is at once a temptation and a clue to speculations which would fill up the blanks which revelation has left, and endeavour, at least, to compact into a psychological system the doctrines which Scripture enunciates as essential to our duty and our salvation. And starting from an idea which the figurative language of holy writ has suggested, it is, perhaps, not a difficult, certainly not an uncongenial task, for the human mind to construct a theory of spiritual influences which may satisfy its desire for logical, or at least, systematic unity, and may, probably, appear solid enough to bear the weight of other inferences, which it would hold and impose as confidently, as if taught by the word of God itself. But though such a theory will accord with certain portions of Scripture,—with those, that is, whose language was its parent, and with their parallels,—it will be found to jar with others, where the truth has been conveyed in other language, or by the medium of different analogies. Hence arises the necessity, if the theory is to be maintained, of explaining away all that is adverse to it,—of commentaries to file down with ingenious industry all the salient angles of divine revelation to a forced accordance with a human system. Wherever recourse is had to this process, it ought to be concluded, that, in reality, the theory has been tried by the word of God, and failed. It was an endeavour to reason out what has not been revealed. The data were insufficient; and the result, when brought to the touchstone of divine truth, is proved unsound.

Let me be allowed the attempt to illustrate this

process by one example out of several. The word *grace* is used occasionally in Scripture, and much more frequently in theology, to express the influence by which the sanctification of man is effected. "My grace is sufficient for thee: for my strength is made perfect in weakness."[1] "Thou, therefore, my son, be strong in the grace," or by the grace, "that is in Christ Jesus."[2] "Let us have," or hold fast, "grace, whereby we may serve God acceptably with reverence and godly fear."[3] But grace means *favour*. This is its radical force, and must run through all its applications. All this is undeniable: and it thus becomes the ground-work for a theory. For the favour of God to man, it is argued, expressed in the redemption of the world by Jesus Christ and revealed in the Gospel, acts upon the moral nature of man as an obligation and a motive; so that he is bound by new and higher sanctions, and urged by fresh impulses of gratitude and affection, to live a life of obedience and holiness. God's grace, therefore, effects man's sanctification only by moral suasion; much as the influence of the truth of the atonement, as a motive, is described from his own experience by St. Paul: "For the love of Christ constraineth us; because we thus judge, that if one died for all, then were all dead; and that he died for all, that they which live should not henceforth live unto themselves, but unto Him which died for them, and rose again.[4]

[1] 2 Cor. xii. 9. [2] 2 Tim. ii. 1. [3] Heb. xii. 28.
[4] 2 Cor. v. 14, 15.

If this be the true theory of grace, there is, of course, no room for any occult supernatural influences or specific action of the Holy Ghost on the human soul. The Gospel covenant does not differ from other dispensations by the imparting of a gift, so much as by a more efficient display of motives. The machinery, so to speak, of our sanctification was all known and employed before; the Gospel does but apply additional power to work it, by revealing the grace or favour of God to man in Christ. Means of grace become, of course, only aids for realizing more effectually the motive thus powerfully unveiled. Sacraments are suggestive of certain facts, truths, motives, and obligations, which ought to be prevalent with every one who receives them, to live according to them; or are representative of his recognition of these truths and his acknowledgment of these motives and duties.[1] There is a simplicity in such a system which to many will appear an evidence of truth; and an entire abrogation of the supernatural, which will be a strong recommendation to all, whom physical studies or a sceptical temperament, have indisposed to the belief of spiritual mysteries. In such eyes, at least, the system will stand well.

But apply the test of Scripture. You may grant that grace means favour, and that it even retains that meaning predominant when it is used of the influence by which man is sanctified. But is *grace* the only,

[1] See Wilson's "Bampton Lectures" for 1851.

or even the ordinary term, by which this influence is expressed? Is not the Holy Spirit more usually spoken of as *Himself* the Agent of our sanctification? Is not language used throughout the whole revelation of the scheme of the Gospel, plainly indicative of the specific action of the Holy Ghost on the human soul? In prophecy, *e. g.* the gift of the Holy Ghost is predicted, as one of the peculiar privileges of the Gospel dispensation? " And it shall come to pass afterward, that I will pour out my Spirit upon all flesh." [1] Our Lord's own promise is even more descriptive of direct and personal influence : " I will pray the Father, and he shall give you another Comforter, that he may abide with you for ever; even the Spirit of truth; whom the world cannot receive, because it seeth him not, neither knoweth him : but ye know him ; for he dwelleth with you and shall be in you." [2]

When this promise was first fulfilled, it was accompanied by sensible effects,—the sound as of a rushing mighty wind, and the cloven tongues like as of fire,—and it sat upon each of the Apostles : symbols, which can hardly betoken anything but a direct supernatural influence, exerted at that moment, and immediately producing its effects in the recipients.

And if it be said, that the Pentecostal effusion was of the nature of a temporary miracle, and belonged only to the extraordinary gifts of the Spirit, it deserves to be considered, how little Scripture re-

[1] Joel, ii. 28.   [2] John, xiv. 16, 17.

cognises the theological distinction between ordinary and extraordinary gifts. In what proportion miraculous endowments were bestowed, or by what rule, we know not: but it was never, I believe, imagined, that all, or even the greater part, of those who were baptized and received imposition of hands, were enabled to speak with tongues, to interpret or to heal. Yet all believers alike are addressed in the Apostolic Epistles as having "received the Spirit,"[1] as having "the earnest of the Spirit,"[2] and as having an "unction from the Holy One."[3] St. Paul classes faith and charity among the χαρίσματα,—more important, indeed, than tongues or prophesyings or the gifts of healing, inasmuch as without these moral graces, we are nothing:—but he does not distinguish them from the miraculous gifts, as to their agent and the nature of the influence by which they were wrought. "To one is given by the Spirit the word of wisdom; to another the word of knowledge, by the same Spirit; to another faith, by the same Spirit; to another the gifts of healing by the same Spirit; to another the working of miracles; to another prophecy; to another discerning of spirits; to another divers kinds of tongues; to another the interpretation of tongues: But all these worketh that one and the self-same Spirit, dividing to every man severally as he will."[4] It is probable, indeed, that, in the minds of the early Christians,

[1] Rom. viii. 15.   [2] 2 Cor. i. 22.   [3] 1 John, ii. 20.
[4] 1 Cor. xii. 8—11.

102　　*Grace : the Personal Agency*

the extraordinary (as we now call them) were divided from the ordinary gifts of the Spirit by a very dim and wavering line; and that their theology would pass from tongues to prophecy, from prophecy to knowledge, from knowledge to faith, and from faith to hope and love, without any distinct consciousness where the miraculous and temporary ceased, and where it was entering that domain of spiritual influence which was to be the Church's heritage for ever. As, therefore, it is, of course, impossible to refer the extraordinary gifts to mere moral causation and the constraining force of motives; as miracles must have been the result of the direct energy of a supernatural power; and as the ordinary graces of the Spirit are exhibited in Scripture as identical with the others in their origin and agent; it can be no mere notion adapted to popular phraseology or bygone modes of thought, but a revealed truth of Scripture, that the moral change wrought in the affections, will, character, and lives of those who are saved, is effected by the direct and personal influence of the Holy Ghost.

And this conclusion is supported by the almost uniform language of Holy Writ, when speaking of spiritual influence. Such influence is an ἐνέργεια, implying an agent, and a result (ἔργον). As the spirit of evil is said to *work* in the children of disobedience;[1] so "it is God," teaches St. Paul, "which

[1] Eph. ii. 2.

worketh (ὁ ἐνεργῶν) in you both to will and to do (ἐνεργεῖν) of his good pleasure."[1] The *works* (ἔργα) of the flesh are opposed, as to a synonym, to the *fruit* of the Spirit:[2] and the flesh, meaning the natural appetites, affections, and corrupt will, is the frequent antithesis of the Spirit, which must therefore imply some specific influence antagonistic to this will. "The flesh lusteth against the Spirit, and the Spirit against the flesh: and these are contrary the one to the other."[3] The chapter from which the text is taken, is full of expressions, which, while they naturally convey the idea of the personal, immediate agency of the Holy Ghost in man's sanctification, cannot, without great violence, be explained on the theory of a mere moral influence of motives. For after contrasting life on carnal principles with life on spiritual principles, and the carnal with the spiritual mind (φρόνημα), the Apostle continues, as it were in explanation: "Ye are not in the flesh, but in the Spirit, if so be (or since) the Spirit of God dwell in you: Now (but) if any man have not the Spirit of Christ, he is none of his. If ye live after the flesh, ye shall die: but if ye, through the Spirit, do mortify the deeds of the body, ye shall live. For" (again defining a more ambiguous expression by words which imply a specific and personal influence) "as many as are led by the Spirit of God, they are the sons of God."[4] Almost immediately, this spiritual

[1] Phil. ii. 13.   [2] Gal. v. 19, 22.   [3] Gal. v. 17.
[4] Rom. viii. 9, 13, 14.

agent is contradistinguished from our own spiritual nature, with which, however, he is co-operating. "The Spirit itself beareth witness with our spirit that we are the children of God."[1] And still further on we read, " Likewise the Spirit also helpeth our infirmities: for we know not what we should pray for as we ought; but the Spirit itself maketh intercession for us with groanings which cannot be uttered,"[2] or unuttered groanings;—words which, difficult, perhaps, in any case, are inexplicable on the hypothesis that all spiritual influence is resolvable into the moral influence of the constraining motives of the Gospel.

It may be said, indeed, that the language of Scripture is not only formed on the phraseology, but accommodated to the ideas of the age when it was revealed, and to the state of knowledge, psychological, no less than physical, which had then been attained: and that, as we find little difficulty in modifying Scriptural statements of natural laws or phenomena by the more accurate science of modern times, so there is no reason why we should not consider the terms by which spiritual influences are expressed as adjusted to the ideas and belief then prevalent, and to be now translated into their equivalents in the present advanced state of mental and moral philosophy. But in the first place, the parallel will not hold, if we take in, as an element in the reasoning, the purpose for which revelation was made. It

Rom. viii. 16.   [2] Ib. ver. 26.

was not its object to instruct us in physical science; and, therefore, statements in that subject matter, which are introduced for the most part by the way and illustratively, need not be accurate, or rather would have defeated their own purpose as illustrations, if they were. But it *is* the object of revelation to instruct us in spiritual things; to make us "wise unto salvation;" and, therefore, to inform us at least of the way and power by which we are sanctified, no less than justified. And such an accommodation to previous systems or prejudices as is here assumed, would not merely abdicate the office of revelation, but would actually make it the instrument of leading us astray. For though the *mode* in which the influence of the Holy Spirit acts on our moral nature, may be of no practical importance, and may therefore be left a mystery; yet the *fact* that He does personally and immediately so act, is one of great moment, and involves, as we may, perhaps, see presently, several weighty consequences.

But further, it begs the very point in question to assume, that modern mental and psychological science has so far solved the phenomena and discovered the laws of man's moral constitution, as to be able to account for the process of the soul's sanctification without the direct influence of a supernatural power. So far is this from being the case, that, even supposing the satisfactory solution of the complicated questions arising from our free will and moral choice, and the attraction of affections and motives, it would still remain a mystery incapable of reduction under any law, why two wills equally free, and under similar conditions, should vary so materially in their choice of ends; and there would still be room for the truth, which Scripture at least *seems* to reveal so distinctly, of the direct intervention of the influence of the Holy Spirit.

And, lastly, the language of holy writ is on this subject so distinct and consistent; it speaks so often and so plainly of the Holy Ghost as an Agent, given to man, dwelling and energising in him; that to treat all such expressions merely as adapted to the understanding and ideas of those in whose age they were employed, would be virtually to eliminate from the word of God all positive and specific meaning, when it speaks of the supernatural, and to forge a key with which any hands who will, may abstract from the treasures of revelation the truths of the Incarnation, the Atonement, or the Trinity.

When, however, we speak of the grace of the Holy Ghost (using grace in its theological, rather than its usual scriptural sense) as a direct influence of the divine Spirit on the heart of man,—it is not meant to imply any theory as to the *mode* of this influence. Theories, indeed, there are, complete enough in themselves, but untenable (like that we have been considering) when placed fairly beside the word of God: and these may form the subject of future examination. The revealed facts respecting man's sanctification are these; God the Holy Ghost the Agent; man's spiritual and moral nature the subject on which He acts; and the result, holiness in all its parts,—from the first conviction that leads to penitence, to the re-creation of "the perfect man, the measure of the stature of the fulness of Christ." There are also provided means, by which man may seek and obtain His aid, and instruments by which He ordinarily works. But the mode of His working, and the metaphysical forces and affinities by which spirit acts on spirit, as we shall probably seek in vain to discover, so we may be well content to be ignorant of. "The wind bloweth where it listeth; and thou hearest the sound thereof, but canst not tell whence it cometh, and whither it goeth; so is every one that is born of the Spirit." [1]

Let it not be supposed, however, that the truth of the special influence of the Holy Ghost in the work of man's sanctification, is merely a speculative point of abstract theology, with little or no immediate bearing on our responsibilities and conduct. Its practical importance will, I hope, be made evident by a few concluding remarks.

1. It is a truth, then, in the first place, calculated, and doubtless intended, to keep us watchful against sin, and jealous of even the approach of evil, that our souls are, as it were, brought into immediate contact

[1] John, iii. 8.

with the holy and eternal Spirit of God. I am not desirous of extenuating the force which the grace of God, taken in the sense of His favour, ought to exercise over us as a motive. That wonderful dispensation of the divine love and mercy to us, the Gospel,—emphatically *the grace* of God,—cannot be really accepted by us as a truth, without awakening thankfulness and endeavour, nor neglected, without gross ingratitude. "The love of Christ" ought, no doubt, "to constrain us to live no longer to ourselves, but to him who died for us and rose again." But mere moral motives are weak to resist passion: and gratitude, even when vivified by the aid of the Holy Spirit, needs to be strengthened and reinforced by other principles of action. And as the truth of the omnipresence of God realised by faith, is a powerful motive against sin, and we fear to offend in the presence of Him,—or more accurately, *in* Him,— "in whom we live and move and have our being;"[1] so the belief of the actual presence of the Holy Ghost acting in and with our spirit,—the awful conviction that the Divinity Himself is working in the mysterious processes of our inner life,— should surely impress us strongly with a dread of sin,—of the inward thought, no less than of the outward act,—and should lead us (as the Apostle argues from the indwelling of God in His people) "to cleanse ourselves from all filthiness both of the flesh

[1] Acts, xvii. 28.

and spirit; perfecting holiness in the fear of God."[1] And I need not remind you of his application of this truth in reference to that class of sins which most of all defile both body and mind; and leave a stain of impurity on the soul, which years of after penitence may mourn for bitterly, but cannot efface. "What, know ye not that your body is the temple of the Holy Ghost which is in you?"[2]

2. Another consequence of the belief that all holiness is the effect of a special influence of the Holy Ghost on the soul, is the growth of true humility. If there is one phase more than another, in which the Gospel stands contradistinguished from all other religions and all systems of philosophy, it is as humbling man, and exalting God. "By grace are we saved through faith; and that not of ourselves; it is the gift of God."[3] As our justification is the act of divine mercy for the merits of Christ justifying the unrighteous: so with respect to our sanctification, "we are his workmanship, created in Christ Jesus unto good works."[4] But if our holiness proceeds from God, only as other good and perfect gifts come from above, from the Father of lights, as the result of the moral laws He has enacted, and the influential motives He has revealed, then is our obedience as much *our* work, as it would be under the law, or any other system whatever. The motives suggested may

[1] 2 Cor. vi. 16—18; vii. 1.   [2] 1 Cor. vi. 19.
[3] Eph. ii. 8.   [4] Eph. ii. 10.

be higher, and purer; but the whole moral process and the determination of the will are, in all the cases alike, our own. And there seems no more reason, on this theory, why the Christian should not claim the merit of his good actions, so far as they are good, than why the Peripatetic or the Stoic should not on theirs. Far different is the teaching of the Gospel. It is not only in the arduous and awful labours of the ministry that "we are not sufficient of ourselves to think anything as of ourselves;"[1] but "apart from Christ we can do nothing."[2] To do good works pleasing and acceptable to God, we need the grace of God by Christ,—the specific influence of the Holy Spirit,—both to prevent us that we may have a good will, and to work with us when we have that good will. And when we are working out our own salvation with fear and trembling, it is God that is working in us both to will and to do of His good pleasure.[3] What room, then, is there for self-gratulation, or the confidence of human merit? "Who maketh thee," asks the Apostle, "to differ from another? and what hast thou that thou didst not receive? Now, if thou didst receive it, why dost thou glory, as if thou hadst not received it?"[4] Much reason, indeed, has the Christian for thankfulness and humble praise in his sanctification; but for self-exaltation, for the complacency of desert, none. The motive, the desire,

[1] 2 Cor. iii. 5.   [2] John, xv. 5.
[3] Phil. ii. 12, 13.   [4] 1 Cor. iv. 7.

the choice, the power, all are given him from above. "Let him that glorieth, glory in the Lord."

3. Finally, it is from realising the truth that a direct influence of the Holy Spirit is exerted in our sanctification, that we obtain confidence to wage the contest against evil, and to "run with patience the race that is set before us." I may appeal to all who have ever made the trial in earnest, and with whom the warfare against the world, the flesh, and the devil is, not a forgotten vow, but a stern reality, whether their heart has not at times failed them, and the damp of despondency fallen on them, as they marked the ebbs and flows of their spiritual life, ever varying, never gaining; as they seemed to be treading the same weary round of purposes unfulfilled and resolutions made and broken; or as they wept over a relapse into some forsaken sin,—forsaken as they had trusted for ever. With what hope can they renew the contest? Their strength has proved unequal to it; their good intentions have soon lost their elasticity and force, or given way under the pressure of temptation; the motives of the Gospel, constraining as they ought to be, have failed to animate and support them. Where shall they find strength? In a power *out* of themselves, brethren, though working in them; even the promised and present influence of the Holy Ghost. It is St. Paul's answer to his own desponding cry, "Wretched man that I am, who shall deliver me from the body

of this death? I thank God through Jesus Christ our Lord."[1] And in a time of trial, when he besought the Lord thrice that the "thorn in his flesh might depart from him," he received the reply, "My grace is sufficient for thee: for my strength is made perfect in weakness."[2]

The same conviction should be our comfort and strength. Past failures have taught us our own insufficiency: but "our sufficiency is of God." In not recognising this truth, or not recognising it as we ought, has probably lain the secret of our ill success. The Almighty is on our side; but we have not sought or valued His aid aright. Henceforth let us continue the contest against evil in the full light of the promises, "Walk in the Spirit, and ye shall not fulfil the lust of the flesh."[3] " Sin shall not have dominion over you, for ye are not under the law, but under grace."[4] "If ye, through the Spirit, do mortify the deeds of the body, ye shall live."[5] Our felt weakness will then be our best strength; for it will oblige us to trust on God: and even past failures will thus lead on to future triumphs. The more simple is our trust, and the more sincere our reliance, on the aid of the Holy Spirit, the more perfectly shall we learn the paradox of the Apostle's experience, "When I am weak, then am I strong:"[6] and if, when the struggle is waxing fainter, and we are nearing the goal, we

[1] Rom. vii. 24, 25. [2] 2 Cor. xii. 8, 9. [3] Gal. v. 16.
[4] Rom. vi. 14. [5] Rom. viii. 13. [6] 2 Cor. xii. 10.

are permitted, like him, to say, as we look back over our soul's inner history, "I have fought the good fight, I have finished my course, I have kept the faith,"[1] it will be our delight to add from the fulness of a grateful heart, "Yet not I, but the grace of God which was with me."[2]

[1] 2 Tim. iv. 7.   [2] 1 Cor. xv. 10.

SERMON VII.

GRACE NOT A QUALITY.

1 Cor. xv. 10.

Yet not I, but the grace of God which was with me.

HOLY SCRIPTURE, honestly applied, is the solvent of human systems of theology. Incapable of embracing the whole circle of divine truth, and yet impatient of imperfection or doubt, the mind of man has a tendency to seize on some one revealed truth, to fix it firmly in its own convictions, and then to cluster other doctrines round it, as a centre, filling up the interstices with its own theories, till it has blended all into the appearance of a consistent whole. The central truth will vary, and the character of the system will vary with it. At one while the unity of the Church; at another, justification by faith alone; at another, the eternal foreknowledge and predestination of God, will be the doctrines to which all the rest are to be forced to subserve. Each alike, as long as we allow ourselves to wrest or pretermit the plain teaching of Scripture, and to substitute logical inferences for the dicta of revelation, will stand with all the appearance of consistency, and the consequent presumption of truth. But it will not abide the test, when every portion of God's word is allowed its due weight, and exhibited in its due proportions. It is but partial truth, and will not coincide with the whole truth;. and exceptions have to be made, and qualifications added, which at last destroy the theory which needs them. The system which has crystallized so symmetrically round some central doctrine, dissolves and disappears, when exposed to the full rays of Scripture light.

This is especially the case, when a theological theory has formed, not so much round a doctrine, as round an idea,— an analogy, for instance, which because it holds good under one point of view, is generalized, and made to apply as a universal truth. The system has a simplicity and oneness which recommends it to our natural love of the complete and definite; but falls to pieces, when placed fairly by the side of Scripture. Thus, because the word grace means favour, it has been inferred that the grace by which the sanctification of man is effected, is but the favour of God to man expressed in the redemption of the world by Jesus Christ and revealed in the Gospel, acting upon the moral nature of man as an obligation and a motive : and a theory results from which the supernatural is eliminated, and which has the double charm of simplicity and the absence of mystery; though it stands in contradiction to the whole tenor of revelation, which attributes the sanctification of man to the personal influence of God the Holy Ghost.

There is another theory connected with the same great work of our sanctification, which exercises a considerable and perhaps unconscious influence over many minds; but which is equally destitute of the corroboration of God's word. In order to express the powerful and continuing effect of the energy of the Holy Spirit on man's moral nature, figures are used, both in Scripture and theology, borrowed from the material world. The seed which takes root, grows, and bears fruit; the fire, which is kindled, and burns; a gift poured out and shed upon those who receive it; are expressive images, without the use of which it would be difficult for divine truths to be conveyed vividly to human comprehension. We read, therefore, "Whosoever is born of God doth not commit sin; for his seed remaineth in him."[1] "Quench not the Spirit."[2] "Wherefore I put thee in remembrance that thou stir up,—$\dot{a}\nu a\zeta\omega\pi\nu\rho\epsilon\tilde{\iota}\nu$—the gift of God, which is in thee by putting on of my hands."[3]

From these and suchlike forms of speech, useful

---

[1] 1 John, iii. 9. [2] 1 Thess. v. 19.
[3] 2 Tim. i. 6.

Grace not a Quality. 117

and, perhaps, necessary for the purposes of revelation, has arisen a theory, in which grace becomes a quality infused into the soul by the Holy Spirit,—a something intermediate between the divine energy of the third Person of the blessed Trinity, and the effects of that energy, repentance, faith, love and obedience,—the renovation of man's moral character. Imparted in baptism, or at conversion (for the theory may be held with modifications in either system), grace is a principle within us; a seed, which may lie dormant for a while, be quickened and grow; a gift, which we may be unconscious of, may neglect and lose, or may cherish, improve, and increase; a faculty, which may be inert and lifeless, but which ought to act and generate the virtues of the Christian character. As the sacraments and apostolic ordinances are means and channels of grace, this quality is conveyed in and by them. It is infused in baptism, strengthened in confirmation, quickened in the Lord's Supper, transmitted by imposition of hands. It is a sacred and mysterious deposit, committed to us to be used, and of which we are to render an account.

It is probable that some such language as this, is necessary in theology; and that it would be difficult to speak long of the influences of the Holy Spirit on the moral nature of man, still more of the duties and obligations they involve, without having recourse to such figures as have given birth to this hypothesis:

but it is one thing to use a phraseology consciously and avowedly as metaphorical, and another, to adopt that language as the expression of a psychological truth, and of the actual mode of the operations of the Holy Spirit. It is one thing to denote and illustrate the development of the moral change wrought by divine grace in the human character, by the figures of a germinating seed, a cherished gift, or a brightening flame; and another, to conceive of divine grace as a certain something in the soul, intermediate between the Agent, who is the Holy Ghost, and the effect, which is the renovation of the moral being,—a something of which the seed, the gift, or the fire, are strictly analogues.

Nor is it merely a speculative question whether such a conception be true or false. It can hardly be, that a theory on such a subject as God's grace and man's sanctification, can be without its influence on our faith and practice; nor, if the theory be unsupported by Scripture, can that influence be other than evil.

In the first place, to imagine grace to be a quality infused in the soul, distinct from, although the result of, the personal influence of the Holy Ghost, has a direct tendency to weaken that sense of the Spirit's personal presence and energy, which is, with the Christian, at once a safeguard against sin, and his support and encouragement under temptation. We know how the too exclusive study of second causes obscures in the mind the practical conviction of the presence and power of the great first Cause, from whose almighty will the spark proceeds which runs through the whole chain to the effect we feel; and that the curious investigator of the laws of nature, of the doctrines of probabilities, and of the principles of human action, is in danger of losing hold of the happy belief that "in God we live and move and have our being;" that "not a sparrow can fall to the ground without our Father; and that the very hairs of our head are all numbered." We may remember that the school of metaphysics, which taught that ideas are a something intermediate between the impression which produced them and the mind which perceives them, instead of states of the individual mind itself, proceeded by an easy process to deny, or doubt, the existence of the external world: for the idea only being the object of which the mind is conscious, what evidence is there of anything beyond? And we may easily conceive, that, without denying the continued personal influence of the Holy Ghost, we may be led practically to forget or undervalue it, by the belief that His grace is something in us, distinct from Himself and from its effects; a mystical deposit which is to be the object of our caution and our efforts. We may neglect the Giver for His imaginary gift.

Again; the theory that grace is a quality intermediate between the heavenly Agent and the effect leads, only too readily, to a semi-materialistic and superstitious doctrine of sacraments. Instead of occasions and instruments by which, ordinarily, the Holy Spirit works, they become vehicles in which grace is deposited, and by which it is conveyed. The water, not merely sanctified to the mystical washing away of sin, and the appointed sign of the death unto sin and a new birth unto righteousness, is the recipient of a mysterious gift, transmitted by it to the soul of the baptized, there, perhaps, to lie dormant for many years, or even to perish altogether unimproved. The consecrated elements are not only effectual signs, so that the souls of those who eat and drink them rightly, worthily, and with faith, are fed with the spiritual reality of the body and blood of Christ, but they are in some ineffable way conjoined with the divine grace; and daring questions are asked, how and when the grace of God comes upon them, and when they cease to be mere bread and wine and become something infinitely more mysterious and holy. The sacraments being thus transmuted into charms, their services are treated almost as incantations. Conditions and limits are assigned, which the word of God has not placed: and the omission of a form or the transposition of a syllable is thought almost as great a bar to their efficacy, as the absence in the recipient of repentance, faith or charity.

It is true, indeed, that the apparent consequences

Grace not a Quality. 121

of a theory, however injurious or however contradictory, are not necessarily subversive of the theory itself, because they may in reality result from its abuse. Holy Scripture is the test of truth. To the law and to the testimony we must bring all human systems, if we would try their pretensions, and decide upon their validity.

Now a careful examination of the apostolic writings will show, it is believed, that there is no trace in them of any quality called grace, or answering to what is *now* called grace, intermediate between the personal energy of the Holy Ghost and the effects produced, whether miraculous, as the gifts of tongues and healing, or moral, as faith, love, hope and charity. In the case of the miraculous gifts, indeed, no such intermediate quality is supposed; and it will be admitted that "holy men of old spake," and prophesied, and cured diseases, "as they were moved by the Holy Ghost." But if the distinction between ordinary and extraordinary gifts was unknown to apostolic times, and has been forced upon the Church only by the event; if the early believers attributed their supernatural endowments, miraculous and moral alike, to the same source, and were unable, perhaps, to conjecture which of the gifts of the Spirit would be continued, and which withdrawn; if St. Paul classes faith not only with "the word of wisdom and the word of knowledge," but also among the gifts of healing and the working of miracles, "as worked by the self-same Spirit dividing to every man severally as he will;"[1] and if he distinguishes charity from tongues and miracles, not as proceeding from a different agent or in a different mode, but only as "a more excellent way;"[2]—it is reasonable to infer, that the moral, no less than the miraculous gifts, are wrought in us by the personal energy of the Holy Ghost, without the interposition of any infused quality called *grace*, which, in the *miraculous* endowments at least, could not even be supposed to exist.

In fact, that which is said in Scripture to be in believers, is not grace, but the God of grace; the Father and the Son by the Holy Ghost, proceeding by the Father and the Son. "I will pray the Father, and he shall give you another Comforter, that he may abide with you for ever: . . . . he dwelleth with you, and shall be in you. I will not leave you comfortless, I will come to you. . . . . My Father will love him, and we will come unto him, and make our abode with him."[3] "Ye are not in the flesh, but in the Spirit, if so be the Spirit of God dwell in you. Now if any man have not the Spirit of Christ he is none of his. And if Christ be in you, the body is dead because of sin, but the Spirit is life because of righteousness."[4] "What! know ye not that your body is the temple of the Holy Ghost which is in you?"[5] "Know ye not your ownselves, how that Jesus Christ is in you, except ye be reprobates?"[6]

---
[1] 1 Cor. xii. 9—11. [2] 1 Cor. xii. 31; xiii. [3] John, xiv. 16. 18, 23.
[4] Rom. viii. 9, 10. [5] 1 Cor. vi. 19. [6] 2 Cor. xiii. 5.

It would be presumptuous alike and unnecessary to attempt in this place any critical examination of the terms used in Scripture, by which the influence and effects of the Holy Spirit are expressed. It will be found, I believe, that the word χάρις, in the comparatively few passages in which it relates to this great instance of the divine favour to man, has always one of two meanings. It either signifies the supernatural influence of the Holy Ghost itself, under the point of view in which it appears as a manifestation of God's free and undeserved mercy; or it is used for the *effects* of that influence, almost synonymously with χάρισμα. Of the former usage the words of the text may serve as an example. "I am the least of the apostles," wrote St. Paul, "that am not meet to be called an apostle, because I persecuted the church of God. But by the grace of God I am what I am,"—that free mercy, which, notwithstanding his unworthiness, had called and enabled him to the work of an apostle by the supernatural aid of the Holy Ghost: "and his grace which was bestowed upon me," or His grace towards me, ἡ χάρις αὐτοῦ ἡ εἰς ἐμέ, "was not in vain," or without its fruits; "but I laboured more abundantly than they all: yet not I, but the grace of God which was with me," ἡ χάρις τοῦ Θεοῦ ἡ σὺν ἐμοί.[1]

Of the latter sense, when χάρις seems used for the *effect* of the supernatural influence of the Spirit, almost as synonymous with χάρισμα, an example is

[1] 1 Cor. xv. 9, 10.

furnished by St. Peter. "As every man hath received the gift, χάρισμα, even so let him minister the same one to another, as good stewards of the manifold grace of God," ποικίλης χάριτος Θεοῦ.[1] And in the second Epistle to the Corinthians it seems to be employed as interchangeable with δωρέα. "Their prayer for you, which long after you for the exceeding grace of God in you," διὰ τὴν ὑπερβάλλουσαν χάριν τοῦ Θεοῦ ἐφ' ὑμῖν. "Thanks be unto God for his unspeakable gift," δωρεᾷ.[2]

It has been said, indeed, that χάρις is applied to the ordinary, and χάρισμα to the extraordinary gifts of the Spirit; but this is a rule which will hardly bear examination. It is doubtful, as has been remarked before, whether the distinction into ordinary and extraordinary gifts existed in the language or ideas of the earliest believers; and by St. Paul[3] the gift of continence is called χάρισμα, as well as those moral graces which are requisite for the due performance of the work of the ministry, "the spirit of power and of love, and of a sound mind."[4] The distinction would rather seem to be, that the term χάρισμα denotes the results of the Spirit's influence more distinctly *as results*—things given; while χάρις expresses them in closer connection with the source—the favour of God from which they proceed; so much so, that it is difficult in several passages to determine, whether the mercy of God which gave, or the gift which resulted

[1] 1 Pet. iv. 10. [2] 2 Cor. ix. 14, 15. [3] 1 Cor. vii. 7. [4] 2 Tim. i. 7.

from His mercy, was the idea most prominent in the writer's mind.

But all I am now concerned to observe is, that of grace, considered as a quality in the soul, intermediate between the Agent, the Holy Spirit, on the one hand, and the effect produced, either as an extraordinary endowment or an ordinary gift on the other, Scripture contains no trace. It is but a theory which has formed round a figure, and has been compacted by the natural desire of the mind for the definite and complete.

The revealed truth appears to be this. Of God's free mercy, and as a consequence of the death, resurrection and ascension of our Lord Jesus Christ, God the Holy Ghost vouchsafes personally to exercise a supernatural influence on the moral, and, possibly, indirectly, on the intellectual faculties of Christians. He is thus said to come to them, to dwell in them, and to work in them. Of the mode of His operation we know absolutely nothing. It takes place in that region of unravelled mystery, our own soul, which, though it can traverse the universe, and decipher its laws and analyse its parts, has never found the mirror which can show itself its own spiritual being. But the *effects* we can discern; conviction of sin, repentance, faith, love, obedience, —the renovation and sanctification of the whole moral character, to which in early times was added, and continued while needed by the exigencies of the infant Church, the power of explaining Scripture, of foretelling future events, of speaking or interpreting languages which had not been learnt, of healing diseases, or of working other miracles;—not universally, indeed, nor perhaps generally, but as "the self-same Spirit divided to every man severally as he would."[1]

Further; we are furnished with certain means of grace, in the right use of which we are permitted to seek, and are assured of receiving, the influence of the Holy Spirit; but the mode in which He works in them remains entirely unrevealed.

Prayer has the promise, that more readily than earthly parents give good gifts unto their children, our "Heavenly Father will give the Holy Spirit to them that ask him;"[2] and social prayer has the special promise, that "where two or three are gathered together in the name of Christ, there will he be in the midst of them."[3]

Holy baptism is "the washing of regeneration;"[4] so that they who are born in sin and children of wrath, are born again of water and of the Spirit into a state of grace and the family of God.[5] They are brought, therefore, within the promised influences of the Holy Ghost, and the effects *ought* thenceforth to be discernible in their hearts and lives. To say, then,

[1] 1 Cor. xii. 4—11.   [2] Luke, xi. 13.
[3] Matt. xviii. 20.   [4] Tit. iii. 5.
[5] John, iii. 5; Gal. iii. 26, 27.

that the seed of grace is implanted in them at baptism, if it be meant to illustrate the truth, that the virtues of the renewed character ought gradually to unfold themselves, as the plant springs, and grows, and blossoms after the seed is sown, is an apt figure and not without warrant of Scripture; but if it be intended, that some supernatural quality is then infused, which may lie dormant, or germinate only in after years, it is a theory of which the foundation will be sought in vain in the word of God. The scriptural evidence of having the grace of God is not the fact of having been baptized, but the fruits of the Spirit in the life. Nay, our adoption and sonship themselves, although undoubtedly conveyed and sealed to us at baptism, are proved, as to their continuance, by the same test, the actual influence of the Holy Ghost upon the soul: "For as many as are led by the Spirit of God, they are the sons of God."[1] And, therefore, though all believers who have been baptized, have been made the children of God, and with reference to their title and their duty may be called so still, yet those only *are* the sons of God in reality and power, in whom the Spirit of God bears witness with their spirit, so that they can cry with affectionate confidence, "Abba, Father." The same inspired pen, which traced the words, "Except a man be born of water and of the Spirit, he cannot enter into the kingdom of God,"[2] wrote also, "Whosoever

[1] Rom. viii. 14.   [2] John, iii. 5.

is born of God," πᾶς ὁ γεγεννημένος ἐκ τοῦ Θεοῦ,—whosoever, having been born again, continues in that state, and therefore not only *was*, but *is*, a child of God,—" doth not commit sin ; for his seed remaineth in him :" his spiritual life has grown, and flourished, and borne fruit : "and he cannot sin," wilfully and habitually, "because he is born of God."[1]

In the Lord's Supper we are privileged to believe, that the souls of those who rightly, worthily, and with faith, eat bread and drink wine in remembrance of Christ, are fed spiritually and really with the body and blood of Christ ; he dwells in them, and they in him ; their souls are strengthened and refreshed; and the branch, thus abiding more closely in the vine, is enabled to bring forth more fruit. By the Sacrament the Holy Spirit works. But to speculate on the mode in which the inward grace coexists with the outward sign, whether by transubstantiation, or consubstantiation, or impanation, or other mysterious real presence *in* the elements, is surely, not only to theorize daringly beyond the limits of revelation, but to bind irreverently in some materialising system the personal energy of the Almighty and eternal Spirit.

To conclude. Of the modes of the Holy Spirit's operation in the soul of man we know nothing. Of grace, considered as a quality intermediate between the Almighty Agent and the effects in the affections and life, infused into the soul and conveyed in the

[1] 1 John, iii. 9.

Sacraments, Scripture is silent. It is but a figure magnified into a theory. But these solemn facts remain. The Christian's moral being, and all the springs and processes of his inner life, should be, at every instant, under the immediate influence of God the Holy Ghost. As real as the air we breathe, this is as necessary to our spiritual, as that to our natural life ; for " if any man have not the Spirit of Christ, he is none of his." And as it is not immediately by the bodily sense we recognise the presence and purity of the vital air, nor by the process of respiration which beats with unconscious regularity within us, but by the vigour of the frame and the buoyancy of the spirits; so by no special manifestations nor felt inward interferences, do we infer the influences of the Holy Ghost, but by purified affections, an obedient will, and a holy life. Most important, then, is the self inspection which demands an account of our growth in the Christian character, the diagnosis of our soul's health. Carefully should we mark, and duly regulate the current of our thoughts, the tension of our devotions, the nature of our habits, the general colour of our words and actions. In deepening penitence and firmer faith, in love more filial and more childlike trust, in the heart which turns more thankfully to its Saviour and affections which rise more frequently to heaven; in humility, and purity, and truth, and meekness, and charity ; we may read the witness of the Spirit,—the fruits which

K

grow along that unseen course of living water which wells from "the rock which is Christ," and which springeth up into everlasting life. But where the spell of the world is still strong, and the sway of the passions prevails; where appetites are indulged freely, or feebly resisted; where prayer is cold, and religion a weariness; where the love of the Saviour touches no responsive chord in the breast, and God may be feared, indeed, as a Master, but is not loved as a Father, where strife, and envy, and bitterness are, even though the garb of religious zeal is over them; where there is pride or ambition, covetousness or indolent ease, self, life's sole object, and heartless indifference to others;—oh, there is need, Brethren, of anxiety, effort, earnest struggling prayer, lest the Spirit, of whose presence and power there is so little evidence, should leave that faithless soul to harden into the most hopeless, wretched being on this side the grave,—a Christian given over to a reprobate mind.

But if we have entered sincerely on the contest against evil, and are resolved to do God's work here on earth, there is unspeakable comfort in the conviction, that God Himself,—the Almighty Spirit,—is working mysteriously, but really, in us; and that his energy is engaged,—though how we know not,—with our wayward affections and our feeble will. In *temporal* trials, in anxiety and sorrow, it is the best and most powerful consolation to realise the presence of

God: and never are the heart's tremors calmed more surely, or tears dried more quickly, or the weight of grief lightened more gently, than when we feel that the Lord is at hand, that the everlasting arms are under us, and that *in* Him we live and move, and have our being. And in *spiritual* trials, — when temptation is rife, and faith is wavering, and our own weakness has been betrayed by too many a fall before,—it is the conviction, not merely that we have a *gift* from God, but that God Himself is with us; that the feeble efforts of our wills are wielded by the omnipotent Spirit; which can enable us to be steadfast and unmoveable, and hopefully to maintain the contest against the world, the flesh, and the devil. Armed with this belief, endeavour conceives fresh vigour, and the lifelong contest is crowned with success. We not only work, but we *work out* our " salvation with fear and trembling; for it is God which worketh in us both to will and to do of his good pleasure." [1]

[1] Phil. ii. 12

SERMON VIII.

GIFTS GIVEN TO PROFIT WITHAL.

1 Cor. xii. 7.

But the manifestation of the Spirit is given to every man to profit withal.

It is hard to conceive how any system of rationalism can consist with the admission of the authenticity of this Epistle.

The Apostle writes to men, whom he believes to be living, and whom he assumes to believe themselves to be living, under a spiritual dispensation. He addresses them, as gifted with supernatural endowments, not for the purpose of persuading them that they possess them, but with a view to instruct them how to use them. Their existence is an admitted fact: the only question is, how they may be best employed; and there is just the same evidence that those converts had, or at least firmly believed themselves to have, certain gifts of the Spirit, as that they came together into one place, for the purpose of eating the Lord Supper.

But further: the gifts were, many of them, of a character, which, though imposture might, under certain conditions, counterfeit, enthusiasm could, under no supposition, imagine. An inward light, revealing doctrines or inflaming emotions, may easily be kindled by the heat of fanaticism. The Prophet may unhesitatingly announce the future under the inspiration of his own distempered brain. But no mental aberration could persuade so many men that they could heal the sick, still less the sick themselves that they were healed; nor could it be fancy which convinced them, that they spoke with tongues which they had never learned, which they whose the language was, understood, and which others whose it was not, by a similar supernatural endowment interpreted. And as the hypothesis of imposture is precluded by the number of the agents and the publicity of the facts, by the certainty of detection, if there was anything to detect, and the evident simplicity and truthfulness of all the circumstances, proved even by the abuses to which the miraculous endowments were subject; it follows, that these spiritual gifts were real supernatural facts, admitted and felt to be such by St. Paul and the whole Corinthian Church.

In the chapter from which the text is taken, the Apostle commences his instructions as to the real purpose and right employment of these supernatural powers, and continues them to the end of the fourteenth chapter. He would not have the Corinthians ignorant concerning spiritual gifts, as they were indeed the more likely to be, not having had the preparatory training of the Jewish dispensation, but being "Gentiles, carried away unto dumb idols even as they were led:" and he lays down, as the first and essential criterion of the presence of the Spirit, the confession of a true faith: for no one, whatever might be his pretensions, who could say ἀνάθεμα Ἰησοῦν, could be speaking by the Spirit of God: while no one could confess, especially in the face of old prejudices, scorn and persecution, that "Jesus is the Lord," Jehovah, the co-essential Son of God, "but by the Holy Ghost." Here was the test by which they were to "try the Spirits whether they were of God," at a time when the very abundance, probably, of supernatural endowments made mere pretence more common and more easy; when "many false prophets were gone out into the world." And as this test was the same in all, so was the Holy Spirit whose presence and power it attested, the same in all. It was not, as the mental habits of polytheism might infer, and even the traditions of philosophy might suggest, that each possessor of miraculous gifts received them from some attendant spirit, some good dæmon to whom his spiritual being had become linked; but that the same one, personal, Spirit, the Almighty and Everlasting, one in the unity of Godhead with the Father and the Son, worked in every one, "dividing to every man severally as He would." But though the Giver is one, His gifts are various; and they were bestowed upon different members of the Corinthian Church, different both in kind and degree. Hence the next rule the Apostle lays down, expresses the purpose of this diversity. The Spirit itself is one; but to each individual the manifestation of the Spirit in its manifold forms, is given for the purpose of profiting the whole Church. And just as for the welfare of the whole body, it is essential that each limb and organ should have its different and peculiar office, so for the edifying of the spiritual society, each member was to possess and use the gifts, which their divine Author had, in His wisdom, allotted him. And this rule, it should be observed, struck at the root of the emulations and jealousies with which the possession of miraculous endowments, in the Corinthian Church at least, was attended. For as each organ of the natural body is, in its place and function, as important as the rest, and "those members which seem to be more feeble are necessary," so each member of the spiritual body, exercising his allotted gifts for the benefit of all, is, in his own position, as needful and as honourable as the rest. While, at the same time, the great duty is involved, that every believer is bound to employ his spiritual endowments, not for private ends or for his own aggrandisement, but for the benefit of others and the general good. "The manifestation of the Spirit is given to every man to profit withal."

Now it has often been inferred from this passage,—and the inference is both important and just,—that not only spiritual gifts, but all endowments mental and bodily, are entrusted to us for the same end,—not to be expended on selfish gratification or our own peculiar interest, but to be exerted for the welfare of others. For the analogy is obviously very close; and not only do men differ in the kind and degree of their various powers,—health, strength, station, temporal possessions, and the infinitely varying vigour, tension, and distribution of the mental faculties,—but there is a mutual dependence, and an interlacing of various needs, so that each has something which others want, and wants something which others have. And hence arises, on the one hand, the inalienable dignity of each one who is doing his duty in his station, however low it may be; and on the other, the obligation on each to live and work, not for himself only, but for others. This is, indeed, but the application in temporal, as the text is the application in spiritual matters, of the great law which binds all society together,—the law of mutual dependence involving the duty of mutual co-operation.

But from this sound inference a further and more perilous step has been sometimes taken; and it has been concluded that endowments which we are to use by the same rule as spiritual gifts, have also the selfsame origin with spiritual gifts: and that all those qualities, by the excess of which men are distinguished from one another, as strength and beauty and memory and judgment and imagination, and the various degrees and admixtures of each, are to be considered gifts of the Holy Spirit. Whether there may possibly be a sense in which this is true, we may inquire presently. But, broadly held and rhetorically taught, such a theory tends to obliterate the clear line which Scripture draws between the spiritually and the carnally minded, between those who are Christ's and those who are none of His. For if intellectual, at least, if not also bodily endowments are gifts of the Spirit, in at all the same sense as are repentance, faith, and love, and holiness, and are spoken of in the same terms and viewed under the same aspect, it is not wonderful if the seal of the Spirit,—the evidence of God's children,—comes to be looked upon as, at least, but a question of degree, and if, in the haze of an undistinguishing terminology, many cherish a vague belief that they are partakers of the divine nature, whose hearts and lives bear none of the impress of the divine character. Where all have gifts of the Spirit, the possession of *the* gift ceases to be an essential or a privilege. And as in systems where all is deity, each part can owe no special allegiance or obligation to any other, and pantheism is the practical equivalent to atheism; so a theory which assumes all to have spiritual endowments, and places all under supernatural influence, has a tendency to absorb the great truth of sanctification by the special action of the Holy Ghost, and to induce a practical indifference to the reality and necessity of divine grace.

Now it must be, not admitted only, but strenuously maintained, that all endowments, bodily and mental, are from God; talents committed to us by Him to be improved. "Every good and every perfect gift is from above, and cometh down from the Father of lights."[1] It may even be, that, in the economy of the undivided Godhead, the distribution of these gifts may be the office of the Holy Ghost, the Lord and Giver of life: though the assertion that it is so, could hardly find sufficient basis in the pages of holy writ. Instances, indeed, there are of special endowments of wisdom or skill bestowed for the performance of certain duties or the discharge of some particular office, of which the Spirit is the agent, and which answer in the old, to some of the χαρίσματα under the new, dispensation. Thus Bezaleel and Aholiab were "filled with the Spirit of God, in wisdom, and in understanding, and in knowledge, and in all manner of workmanship," for the construction of the tabernacle and its furniture.[2] The Spirit rested on the seventy elders who were to be the coadjutors and council of Moses, and they did prophesy.[3] God gave Saul another heart, when he was anointed to be king over Israel.[4] And even the great bodily strength of Samson was exerted "when the

[1] James, i. 17. [2] Exodus, xxxi. 2, 3.
[3] Numbers, xi. 24—26. [4] 1 Sam. x. 9.

Spirit of the Lord came mightily upon him."[1] But there is, perhaps, hardly enough in such exceptional and extraordinary cases to warrant us in concluding, that, in general, bodily and mental endowments are to be considered gifts especially of the third Person of the blessed Trinity, or that the distribution of *them* to every one severally as He will, is His peculiar office in the divine economy.

But however this may be, it is at least clear, that such endowments ought to separated by a very broad and definite line from that work of the Spirit in the soul of man, which is the witness of our sonship and the earnest of our inheritance. Those are entrusted, varying in degree and kind, to some; this is required, and should be found, in all. Those are but relative goods, to withhold which may often be a greater blessing than to give them: this is of all goods the best, promised to all who seek, and which all must seek to have. Those are consistent with, and sometimes the instruments of, wilful sin: this is holiness itself, planted in the heart and bearing fruit in the life. Those are not necessary, nor always conducive, to salvation: but without this we are none of Christ's and no man can see the Lord. For this, indeed, as essential to present sanctification and future safety, even the extraordinary and miraculous gifts of the Spirit could be no substitute. Samson's endowments did not preserve him from deadly sin, nor Saul's

[1] Judges, xiv. 6.

special gift from final reprobation. And " many will say unto me in that day," said the Judge of all, " Lord, Lord, have we not prophesied in thy name? and in thy name have cast out devils? and in thy name done many wonderful works? And then will I profess unto them, I never knew you: depart from me, ye that work iniquity."[1] Still less can intellectual powers however eminent,—the most brilliant lustre of creative genius, or penetration which can analyse the structure of a universe,—stand on the same ground, as regards our relation to God and our eternal salvation, with the renewal of the moral character by the Holy Spirit, our re-creation after his own image in righteousness and true holiness.

The distinction is so plain, that to state it may seem little more than to elaborate a trite truism. Yet, plain as it is, it may easily be overlooked under the cover of that vague mysticism which is the correlative of rationalistic tendencies, the shadow which they project. And when it is commonly said, that it is the Spirit of God who nerves the strong arm of labour and brightens the eye of health, who fires the poet's genius, and animates the thoughts of the philosopher, who decides in the judgment, recalls in the memory, and pictures in the imagination; when all alike are thus, in their degree, considered as thinking and acting under the influence and with the powers of the Holy Spirit, there is great danger,—notwith-

[1] Matt. vii. 22, 23.

standing the substratum of truth which underlies such unqualified statements—that men will accept the possession of natural endowments in place of the renewing energy of the Holy Ghost, and will be satisfied that they have His influence in their intellect, without looking for His sanctifying power in their heart. And I shall cheerfully bear the blame of combating imaginary perils (which, however, I believe to be real) if I can persuade, with God's blessing, any of my hearers to be content with nothing, as the evidence of the presence of God's Spirit with them, less than the renovation of the whole inner life:—conviction of sin ripened into practical repentance; trusting, living faith in the Lord Jesus Christ; love, the reflexion of God's love to us, glowing towards Him and all who are His; the habitual efforts of a cheerful, but self-denying obedience,—cheerful *because* self-denying; and the result of all, a growing conformity to God, revealed in the example of Him who is "God manifest in the flesh," to be like whom is our profession and duty here, and will be the happiness of heaven.

At the same time no truth can be more important, than that by which the theory we have been considering, has been fallaciously supported, but which is itself rightly deduced from the words of the text. All our endowments, no less than the manifestation of the Spirit, "are given to every man to profit withal." Even without the precepts of revelation, this lesson is taught us by our position in God's world. Built up in a social fabric which is maintained by the mutual coherence of its many parts; woven into the complicated network of society, so that we cannot act without acting upon others in every direction; we may, indeed, if we will, (for we are free agents,) live for ourselves, and employ our powers only on selfish ends; but we are condemned, if we do, by the very conditions of our own existence, and transgress the obvious law of our being.

And in Scripture the same law is re-enacted, with fresh relations, and a more emphatic sanction. Within the great society of the human race, though ultimately to be co-extensive with it, is established another brotherhood, purchased by the blood of Christ, called out of the world by grace, and bound together in union with the one Head of the Church by the inward bond of a common faith, and the outward symbol of the same sacraments. By the law of our first birth, then, we are to live for our fellow-men; by the law of our second birth, especially for our fellow-Christians. "The body," we are, "of Christ, but members in particular." And as the eye sees not for itself, but for the body; and the ear hears not for itself, but for the body; and the foot supports and moves the whole frame to which it belongs; so are the Christian's faculties, whatever they may be,—his powers of body and mind, his time, opportunities, wealth, station, influence, and example,—to be employed, according to the law of his creation and redemption both, to " do good unto all men, especially unto them who are of the household of faith."[1]

It is melancholy to observe the point where the analogy fails between the works of God and the duties of men. The members of the natural body, each perform their allotted functions in the well-compacted economy of the whole, with undeviating, for the most part, and unfelt regularity. The members of the spiritual body, bound to employ their various powers for the common good, are found to misuse them to individual gratification and selfish end, and even to turn them against those whom they were to profit withal.

These words may, perchance, fall upon the ears of some, who are making health and strength,—those invaluable instruments for God's service and man's good,—the mere panders to bodily gratification, the means of running further than others into the excess of riot, without paying the penalty which excess exacts from most; or who recklessly unrein their powers of wit and sarcasm, ridiculing profane and sacred things alike, and scattering sparks of evil, perhaps, in many a breast, to smoulder in uneasy doubt, or to break forth hereafter into open unbelief; or who misuse the fascination of a frank and winning manner, or even the influence,—the mighty influence,—of a generous and loving heart, to draw the inexperienced

[1] Gal. vi. 10.

from the strait path of duty into idleness, and dissipation, and vice; or who waste the faculties which God has given them,—now at the very seed-time of the future harvest, and amidst opportunities which life can never recall, and which eternity may regret, —in aimless indolence or self-indulgent sloth. Surely there is guilt in this, Brethren; differing in degree, perhaps, in each, but still great guilt in all. Our gifts, whatever they may be, are " given to every man to profit withal:" but, instead of profiting, you are, at the best, hiding your talent, and robbing your Lord of His usury; if you are not turning His precious gifts against the Giver, beating the implements of your service into the arms of rebellion, and, instead of " profiting " those whom divine providence has made your neighbours, perilling, either wilfully or recklessly, their souls' salvation and your own.

Nor can those habits altogether escape a similar condemnation, which are one great snare of an age of refinement, and which men admire, perhaps, and mistake for virtue and religion,—habits of social and literary ease. I know how much there is that is amiable and engaging in these, and that to do no harm is a right step onward in a world which lieth in evil. I know that the allotted work of many is among home duties, and that their gifts are employed faithfully to profit withal, without passing beyond that little circle: nor would I deny, that in retirement and leisure, piety and devotion may often flourish and strengthen in their heavenward growth. But is there not danger, that powers, capable of conferring, and therefore intended to confer, great benefits on our brethren and the Church of Christ, may be left to slumber amidst the quiet enjoyment of literary leisure; and that a life, envied by others, and not without its gratifications, may be as profitless, and not much less selfish, than that of the covetous or of the voluptuary? Here, indeed, in the pursuits of learning and science, intellect trains its faculties and finds its weapons. But he would be an ill workman who was ever sharpening the tools he never used; nor would he be worthy of a warrior's name, who sate at home, while the enemy was in the field, polishing over again his untried armour, and pleased with the graceful drooping of his plume. And when God has given powers of genius to discover, or of reasoning to defend, or of imagination to illustrate the truth: where there are faculties and personal endowments, no less than station and opportunities, to influence, to persuade, to originate or advance plans of good, and to carry on God's work of regenerating and blessing this fallen world; and all are allowed to terminate in the tranquil enjoyment of aimless, and, perhaps, desultory study, or are concentrated with misplaced industry on some trifling and fruitless object: it can hardly be without misgiving and uneasy fear that the approach can be regarded of that awful day, when the hidden talent will condemn its

L

owner, and when not to have done good will rank the careless, indolent, and self-indulgent, on the left hand of the Judge, together with the workers of iniquity.

But probably we all need,—if the preacher is not uncharitable and presumptuous in inferring from the facts of his own consciousness the wants of those who are far above him in the spiritual life,—a deeper and more present conviction of our responsibility to God for all the gifts with which He has entrusted us, and of our obligation to employ them in His service and for the good of His Church and people. We need a practical belief of the truth, that God "hath set us as members every one of us in the body, as it hath pleased Him," to perform our allotted office, as well and perfectly as we can, not for ourselves only, but for the whole body, and for Him, its Head. Were it not so, there would be less time wasted, and fewer opportunities lost; less *loitering* through life,—the pregnant source of present dissatisfaction and future regret,—and more of that happy energy, which is emphatically its own reward, which having set a right end before it, pursues it heartily and cheerfully, and "whatever the hand findeth to do, does it with its might."[1]

Such convictions should be deepened, and such belief should be vivified, by the meditations of the present season; when, while preparing to com-

[1] Eccles. ix. 10.

memorate the first Advent, we are led by the Church to look forward to the second Advent of our Lord. Before us is placed to-day that awful time, which the lapse of another year must have brought so much nearer, and which *may* be *very* near, when " there shall be signs in the sun, and in the moon, and in the stars; and upon the earth distress of nations, with perplexity; the sea and the waves roaring; men's hearts failing them for fear, and for looking after those things which are coming on the earth: for the powers of heaven shall be shaken. And then shall they see the Son of man coming in a cloud, with power and great glory."[1] And why will He come? To reckon with His servants;—to reward or punish, according to the use they have made of the talents delivered unto them; and to condemn not merely the rebellious, but the slothful, not only those who have done evil, but those who have not done good for His sake. Let us often place ourselves, and all our plans, pursuits, and habits, in the light of that tremendous day. Let us endeavour to feel now, as we must feel then; and to weigh pleasures and pains, duties and temptations, good and evil, in the balance of the last great judgment. O, how worthless then,— the broken toys of the childhood of our being,—will be most of the objects which engross us now! And to have employed faithfully even one of God's gifts to profit withal; to have done good for Christ's sake

[1] Luke, xxi. 25—27 : Gospel for Second Sunday in Advent.

to Christ's brethren; yea, to have "given to drink unto one of His little ones a cup of cold water only in the name of a disciple,"[1] will be a recollection infinitely more precious, than to have enjoyed to the full even the purest of the world's pleasures, and honours which may be borne without a blush. It may inspire an humble hope (which those could not) that to us may be addressed the transporting words, "Well done, good and faithful servant, enter thou into the joy of thy Lord."[2]

[1] Matt. x. 42.   [2] Matt. xxv. 23.

SERMON IX.

GRIEVING THE SPIRIT.

Ephes. iv. 30.

And grieve not the Holy Spirit of God, whereby ye are sealed unto the day of redemption.

The difficulties arising from the metaphorical language which expresses the divine attributes and operations by terms belonging to human passions and acts, are, perhaps, rather theoretical than practical. Much has been ably said and acutely written to discriminate the line where the analogy fails, and, indeed, becomes a contradiction, when anger, vengeance, repentance, grief, and the like, are attributed to the Deity; and it may be well to guard against the tendency to anthropomorphism, which, by degrading the conception of God, inevitably lowers the moral standard, and weakens the best motives of man. But, after all, the great want of our nature is a vivid conviction of a personal and present Deity; not as a great abstraction, which, however logically correct, the best-trained minds can with difficulty realise, and which is wholly inoperative on the untaught; not veiled under the enigmas of a mystical theology, in which every attribute personified becomes itself a deity, and which ramifies into polytheism and multiform superstition; but, represented to us under forms of thought, and in modes of action, which belong to our idea of a Person, and which, being borrowed from the moral constitution of *man*, are, after all, the highest and noblest images which our present experience can supply.

Now this want the language of the Holy Scripture is adapted with admirable wisdom to meet. So revealing God in His essence as to place an immeasurable distance between Him and man,—as a Spirit, the self-existent I Am, who changes not, with "whom is no variableness, neither shadow of turning,"[1] "who only hath immortality, dwelling in the light which no man can approach unto; whom no man hath seen, nor can see;"[2] it yet unhesitatingly expresses His attributes and relations towards us by every affection, passion, and act, which belongs to man; throws Him, (if the word may be pardoned,) in projecting Him and His dealings with us on the page of revelation, into every attitude which a Person and moral agent, like ourselves, can assume. Nor can we doubt, that He, by whose inspiration all Holy Scripture was written for our learning, would have us feel towards Him, as towards a personal and present Deity,—no

[1] James, i. 17.   [2] 1 Tim. vi. 16.

mere infinite and omnipresent essence of which we and all things form a part,—but a Being other than ourselves (albeit by Him we and all things consist) who acts on us and we on Him, mysteriously, doubtless, but, for all practical purposes, really, in all the relations of which our moral constitution is capable.

We need not be too solicitous, then, to explain away, or to guard till we exclude, such passages as those of the text; " Grieve not the Holy Spirit of God, whereby ye are sealed unto the day of redemption." Metaphysically, indeed, we know that grief, vexation, change, are incompatible with the essence of Deity ; but we should know also, that, practically, our guilt and its consequences, when we commit wilful sin, are exactly the same as if they grieved, vexed, and provoked the departure of that Holy Being, whose special influence on the heart and life is God's seal, identifying those who are His. And as practical holiness, rather than metaphysical accuracy, is that by which we are to be judged, it is of course essential, that in ascertaining the latter, the former should not for a moment be postponed or overlaid.

It is in this practical point of view that I would place the words of the text: but it may be well to observe, first, how far the expression of Holy Writ before us agrees with certain theories of spiritual influence which are afloat in the Church of our days, and to which we have from time to time alluded.

Now it would appear, I think, to be totally inconsistent with that system which would make grace to be but the favour and love of God, especially as manifested in the Gospel, acting potentially as a motive on the affections and will of man. The words do not imply the weakening of a motive, but the offending of a person; nor is it the grace of God which will be obscured or enervated, but the Holy Spirit of God who will be grieved, by sin.

Neither do these words give any support to the notion, that there is a certain quality in the soul we call grace, a something interposed between the personal agency of the Holy Spirit, and the effects, emotions, and virtues, which are the products. They rather exclude it by pointing only to the divine Agent, and to the seal, which, as God's mark on those who are His, must be some perceptible effect, not an occult quality, which could be no distinctive evidence at all.

And they would cease to be applicable on the vague and perilous theory, that all our gifts, our bodily and mental endowments, are, in the same sense as the virtues of the Christian character, graces or gifts of the Spirit: for these are not, directly at least, and frequently not even indirectly, affected even by wilful and habitual sin. On this hypothesis the seal would not be broken; there would be no signs and shrinkings of an offended benefactor.

On the other hand, the expressions of the text fall in with the Church's doctrine of the Personality of the Holy Ghost. And though it would be manifestly unsafe to build such a tenet on a single passage which is necessarily metaphorical, we feel at once the greater propriety of the language, "Grieve not the Holy Spirit of God," when we have inferred His personality from such portions of Scripture as place Him, although in unity with, yet in mysterious contradistinction to, the other persons of the Godhead, as proceeding from the Father, and sent by the Son from the Father, as performing personal offices, as making intercession for us, as leading, speaking, reproving, searching, and as joined with them in those solemn forms, the formula of baptism and the Apostolic benediction, in which Jehovah, the One God, reveals Himself in the light of the new dispensation, as being in the unity of the Godhead three Persons, of one substance, power, and eternity, the Father, the Son, and the Holy Ghost.

On the whole the doctrine of Scripture would appear to be, that the eternal and almighty Spirit, the third Person in the blessed Trinity, exercises a special influence on the moral constitution,—the motives, and affections, and will, and consequently the actions and habits, of man; that by this influence He is said, in an intelligible sense, to be with us, or in us, to dwell in us, and to work in us; that the evidence of this influence, or, in other words, of His presence, is the effect wrought, the moral change which results,—the conviction of sin; godly sorrow issuing in the conversion of heart and life; a cordial reception of the Saviour with all His offers and in all His offices; a cheerful surrender of self and the selfish will to God and His service; "love, joy, peace, longsuffering, gentleness, goodness, faith, meekness, temperance:"[1] and that this presence of the Spirit, thus witnessed by effects which man, unassisted, cannot produce, and the spirit of evil would not and could not counterfeit, becomes the evidence of our justification, the pledge of our adoption, the earnest of our future inheritance,—in a word, the seal of God on His elect, "whereby they are sealed,"—marked with His badge and cognizance which is holiness, and avouched to be His,—" unto the day of redemption:" finally, that the Holy Spirit may be "grieved;" that we may,—speaking, doubtless, metaphorically, and in language properly applicable only to man, but in a sense which is very real, and to be acted upon as unhesitatingly as if we were able to comprehend and express the true relations of human conduct to the Deity,—that we may displease Him, vex Him, provoke Him to withdraw His influence and to depart from us, and thus may break and obliterate that seal, which alone will be man's safety at the Lord's coming.

This is a very solemn truth, which it will be worse than idle to dwell on without casting the eye of the soul inward, and questioning seriously each his own inner self. Born into a world which lieth in the evil

[1] Gal. v. 22, 23.

one, and by nature children of wrath, we have been born again of water and of the Spirit into the family of God, gifted with the privileges of children, and brought within the influences of His grace. His Spirit, therefore, should be with us, and His seal be upon us; and it is a question in which we *must* each be interested, and which we can only escape by virtually confessing the charge from which we shrink: Have I grieved, am I grieving, the Holy Spirit of God?

1. There is one way of doing this so obvious, that conscience can hardly falter in giving in her verdict. Gross and wilful sin, though in some forms the world condones it easily and with a smile, is so palpably evil, that no Christian, in the lowest degree enlightened by Christianity, can give way to it, without experiencing the pleadings and resisting the strivings of the power within. You know some of you, brethren, the misery of that hour,—the first time of yielding to deadly sin; when you had parleyed with temptation, and silenced conscience with what you felt at the time to be a fallacy, and inclination was indulged or passion let loose, till you awoke from the delusion to find that you had been cheated with a lie, and that you were degraded in your own eyes and in the scale of God's creation. But, worst of all, the Holy Spirit was grieved,—shocked (so would He have us deem of Him) as the pure-minded are by sights and sounds of evil. And if by any (which God

forbid!) those sins have been repeated often and have become habitual, and the struggle is little felt, and shame is overlaid by a callous recklessness, it is not that the Spirit is grieved no longer; it is that He has been provoked to depart. The most awful, the most hopeless, of all states on this side the grave, is the peace of habitual and hardened transgressors. It is the silence of a desecrated and deserted temple. The seal is broken, the shrine is empty, the Deity is gone. "Solitudinem faciunt, pacem appellant."

I need hardly say (though I dare not omit it), that of no class of sins is this more true, than of sins of impurity, in deed, or word, or thought. Very strikingly, and alas! not needlessly, has Christianity compassed the grace of chastity with safeguards, and armed it with motives, such as no other religion ever knew. To pollute that body, which the eternal Son of God has hallowed by assuming it and joining it to His own divinity, in which He suffered for our sins, with which He sits at the right hand of the Majesty on high, and with which He will return at the last day to judgment; to defile that frame which is not only part and parcel of our complex self here,—the being who is on his probation for eternity,—but which is to be raised again to be a portion of self for ever, the habitation and the partner of the soul, to share its everlasting bliss or to participate its never-ending misery; this is a sin before which the wildest passion should stand in check; these are thoughts which should make us dread the stain of impurity as a plague-spot, and watch with a holy wariness to keep our bodies in temperance, soberness, and chastity. But even more awful is the motive supplied by the truth before us. Sins which shame the human eye, are done in the presence of the Holy God. *His* shrine is polluted; His Deity outraged; His body defiled. It is the Apostle's argument; I dare not express it but in his own inspired words. " Know ye not that your bodies are the members of Christ? Shall I then take the members of Christ, and make them the members of an harlot? God forbid! What! know ye not that he which is joined to an harlot is one body? for two, saith He, shall be one flesh. But he that is joined to the Lord shall be one spirit. Flee fornication. Every sin that a man doeth is without the body; but he that committeth fornication, sinneth against his own body. What! know ye not that your body is the temple of the Holy Ghost which is in you, which ye have of God, and ye are not your own? For ye are bought with a price: therefore glorify God in your body and in your spirit, which are God's."[1]

2. But there are other ways of grieving the Holy Spirit, as certainly, though less flagrantly. Neglect provokes as much as opposition: and it is no strain on the analogy implied in the text to infer the displeasure of the divine Being and the withdrawal of

[1] 1 Cor. v. 15 – 20.

His sanctifying influence, where there is that habitual disregard of Him, which, displayed among men and towards our earthly benefactors, is justly branded with the charge of ingratitude. And yet it is so true as scarcely to require mention, that multitudes of Christians grow up from baptism and within the pale of the Church, neither unsound in faith nor immoral in life, without any conscious recognition of the Spirit's presence and of their own obligations, without felt penitence, lively faith, or any effort to obey *because* they are God's, the purchase of the Saviour's blood, and the temple of the Holy Ghost. Their realities,—the objects and motives by which they live, —are the things of this world,—its amusements and pleasures, its business and competitions, its honours and profits, its affections, ties, interests, and hopes. All this is sufficiently definite and present to engage the attention, occupy the thoughts, and animate endeavour. With this there is often a vague, and, because vague, inoperative, sense of religious duty, sufficient probably to secure a decent respect for God's word and ordinances, a habit of formal and unfelt prayer, and occasional misgivings as to the adequacy of such religion, and the safety of the soul; but not sufficient to stir the affections, to kindle devotion, or to make head, as a motive, against the strong stream of worldliness and selfishness. And yet that cold, unreal Christian, has been set apart and consecrated " as an habitation of God through the Spirit ;" has had the

Grieving the Spirit.

strivings within him of the power which recreates in the image of God, and should have that seal of holiness on him, which is the earnest and pledge of an eternal inheritance, before which the world pales its transitory and unsatisfying treasures. But he would not have it so. He preferred the world's beaten track, shrunk from effort and self-denial, and almost, perhaps, unconsciously, turned away from the spiritual realities which from time to time placed themselves before him. Neglect has grieved the Holy Spirit. His influence may be withdrawn. And then, the worldly heart elaborates with fearful rapidity from its own inner workings a crust of habitual and callous selfishness, on which all the motives of the law and the gospel alike, the love of the Redeemer and the terrors of the judgment, are expended in vain.

3. Probably the point from which we are most accustomed to view the sin of grieving the Spirit, is that of tampering with and resisting conscience. And with reason; for conscience, informed by revelation, is the organ of the Spirit's pleading in the soul. When, then, we act directly against the dictates of conscience, either impelled by passion, or deliberately choosing what appears expedient instead of what we know to be right, we do in the most daring, and, therefore, the most deadly way, resist and grieve the Holy Spirit of God. But it is seldom, perhaps, comparatively, that conscience is thus openly defied. It is more usual to try to satisfy and silence it by some

plausible fallacy. The appetites and affections have at their command a never-failing supply of ingenious special pleading, which, applied to a present temptation, would take it out of the class of prohibited indulgences, would justify it as necessary, or even advance it to the rank of a duty. It extenuates the guilt of compliance, exaggerates the inconveniences of denial, persuades, perhaps, that the interest of others are involved in our choice, and that charity requires what integrity might have seemed to condemn; or, at least, if beaten from all other wards, suggests that this indulgence will be the last, and, because the last, pardonable, and will be followed by the stern exercise of habitual self-control. Now the soul feels all this to be a sophism. It knows that there is a clear voice calling to the path of duty, and saying, "This is the way, walk ye in it, when it would turn to the right hand, or when it would turn to the left." But it does not desire to hear it. It wants to find a reason for doing wrong. It will even, like Balaam, inquire of the Lord, and pray to be directed, when it has already virtually made its choice. And it is one of the most awful laws of God's moral government, that those who wish to be deceived, will be deceived. They are allowed to cheat themselves with a self-imposed lie. They call evil good, till evil *is* their good. They resist conscience under the plea of respecting it, and have all the guilt, though they may not have the appearance, of grieving the Holy Spirit of God.

4. But, on the other hand, the Spirit may be grieved, where there is a tender, and even a scrupulous, conscience. For it is most important and instructive to observe, as we read the mysterious pages of the human heart, partly in the experience of others, but principally in our own, what a high degree of moral sensitiveness is compatible with spiritual, intellectual, and even lower forms of, pride. There are many who would shrink from the least stain of wilful guilt, and who are honestly obedient to the directions, and even to what they only suspect to be the directions, of conscience, who have admitted and cherish this master passion; and who, while all is fair without, and much is right within, feed sweetly in secret on the consciousness of their own superior endowments of body and mind, of their freedom from error and emancipation from prejudice, of their consummate judgment or their honest love of truth, or of their enjoyment of God's favour, their advance in the spiritual life, and the special manifestations of His grace. Now nothing is more hostile than such a habit to the influences of God's Holy Spirit. "He resisteth the proud, but giveth grace to the humble."[1] To be converted and to become as little children lies at the very threshold of the kingdom of heaven. And where pride sits enthroned under any, even the most godlike, of its forms, the temple may be swept and garnished, it may be adorned with many a grace

[1] James, iv. 6.

and hung with the trophies of many a conquered vice: but the Spirit of God is grieved; His shrine is usurped; He will not inhabit there.

And may it not be asked,—not in the spirit of judging others, lest we should fall into the sin against which we are being warned, but as a caution for ourselves,—may it not be asked, whether we have not here the solution of that perplexing problem, when a pure life, and an earnest piety, and a self-denying charity, have not preserved from gross and perilous error, so that some have been tempted to sever, what is indissolubly united in the oneness of the Godhead, the spirit of holiness from the spirit of truth? May it not be, that if we admit a secret habit of pride, and it becomes (as how soon it does!) dominant in the soul, the Holy Spirit is grieved; His influence is withdrawn; He guides no longer into the whole truth; human ignorance, tricked as spiritual wisdom, assumes the leader's place; and those very faculties on which, perhaps, the heart most prided itself, become the instruments of its fearful punishment? It may be so. At any rate, let us beware. An unaffected, pervading humility, is the handmaid of the Spirit and the Christian's safety; but let " him that thinketh he standeth, take heed lest he fall."[1]

And now, brethren, if by the application of these, or any such-like tests, we should be led to fear that we may have grieved that Holy Spirit of God whereby

[1] Cor. x. 12.

we should be sealed unto the day of redemption, let us not shrink from probing the wound, which, unhealed, is fatal. Let us trace out the cause, confess it sorrowfully, and unsparingly remove it. It is worth any sacrifice to restore the desecrated temple to its rightful Lord. But let us not forget that the Gospel is a remedial scheme, a dispensation of mercy; and that while it condemns our sin, it opens the way to pardon and restoration. It is not because we have grieved the Spirit, that, therefore, we have had our trial, and our salvation is well-nigh hopeless. God forbid! Our guilt is indeed great: but if we feel that guilt and mourn for it; if we are yearning for pardon, and earnest for holiness; if we would be again the temples of the Holy Ghost, and have the seal reset upon us; then is He working in us now, wakening desires which stir not in the reprobate mind, and prompting prayers which are never heard in the shrine deserted by the Deity. Pray fervently for the pardon of the past, and for grace for the future. Trust for the first to the all-sufficient merits of the Redeemer and the infinite mercy of God reconciled to us in Him: look for the last to the never-failing fount of divine grace and the unlimited promises to faithful and persevering prayer. "Ask, and it shall be given you; seek, and ye shall find; knock, and it shall be opened unto you. If ye, being evil, know how to give good gifts unto your children; how much more shall your heavenly Father give the Holy

Spirit to them that ask Him?"[1] Above all, live warily; as those who have a treasure which carelessness will endanger, and wilful sin forfeit; as those to whom "God hath said, I will dwell in them and walk in them," and who dare not, and would not if they dared, grieve the present and holy Spirit of God.

It is He, remember, by whom we are sealed unto the day of redemption: and "now is our redemption nearer than when we believed."[2] It matters little how we interpret the mystical page of unfulfilled prophecy, nor what is our theory concerning "that day and that hour which no man knoweth, no not the angels of heaven, but the Father only."[3] Whatever be its date or character, it is coming; and "suddenly as a thief in the night." And when that day breaks upon the trembling universe, they only will be owned as the Lord's whom He comes to receive unto Himself, who have the seal upon them,—the seal of the Spirit, which is holiness. O thought to animate watchfulness and kindle the fervency of prayer! *We* have been sealed. The promise of the covenant is ours, and the strivings of the Spirit have been within us. The fruits and evidence should be felt in our hearts, and seen in our lives. But what if wilful disobedience or impurity have grieved the Holy Spirit of God; if neglect and worldliness; if we have

---

[1] Luke, xi. 9—13.   [2] Rom. xiii. 11.
[3] Matt. xxiv. 36.

tampered with conscience, by whose voice He spoke; or provoked Him by cherished pride of heart? And if the day bursts upon us impenitent and unpardoned? God save us from the hopeless horror of that moment which enwraps eternity,—when the Lord has come, and has found the seal broken!

SERMON X.

THE DISCERNMENT OF SPIRITUAL THINGS.

1 Cor. ii. 14.

But the natural man receiveth not the things of the Spirit of God: for they are foolishness unto him: neither can he know them, because they are spiritually discerned.

In prosecuting the exercise of self-examination and consequent humiliation which are the especial duties of Lent,[1] it will be a serious error to confine the search to those habits which are more strictly termed moral. Our intellectual habits, too, should be brought before the bar of conscience, to be interrogated, and, if need be, condemned and repented of. Every deeper analysis of our inner constitution tends to show, that no broad distinction between these two species of habits considered in their origin, however necessary for the purposes of classification, can be scientifically maintained. The will enters, though with different inten-

[1] Preached on the 4th Sunday in Lent, 1854.

sities and in different periods of their process, into each. Each is modified indefinitely by external circumstances: each acts and re-acts in a thousand complicated relations on the other: and so entwined together are the fibres of their growth and being, that they cannot be discriminated till that great day, when the human will, bared, in the gaze of omniscient Justice, of all that distracts and bewilders our judgment here, stands out to be sentenced before the tribunal of God.

And there are two reasons why he, who, in the shade and silence of this solemn season, would gain a true knowledge of himself in order to that abasement which is the groundwork of pardon and holiness, will be especially anxious to examine his intellectual habits: the one, because these, being less obviously the product of the will, are apt to grow up unnoticed, and rarely, even if wrong, can cause that monitory start and pang of conscience which is consequent on an act or thought of merely moral evil. The other, because these habits are, at least as to the character of its creed, the mould and matrix of our faith; which, to be saving, must not only be of the pure metal of sincerity, but bear the genuine impress of divine truth.

Of all evil intellectual habits, beyond compare the most universal and subtle is that of intellectual pride. Entering, as it seems to have done, into the inducements of the primal sin, when man, who knew enough for duty and happiness, would be as gods, knowing good and evil, it has reappeared throughout the world's history, wherever mind has emerged from the mere animal life of barbarism, adapting itself to the various phases and degrees of human knowledge, and becoming epidemic under various shapes. It has found its congenial, though often fantastic expression, in almost every form of human philosophy; in the Pantheism of the Buddhist and the Brahmin, no less than in the self-conceited subtleties of the Stoic, and the far nobler desire and emulation of the Godlike, which was taught in the Academy and the Lyceum. In the Church it has been the prolific parent of innumerable heresies, from the grotesque blasphemies of the Gnostics and all the graduated shades of early antitrinitarian error, to the systematized self-sufficiency of the schoolmen, and the cold and motiveless creed of the followers of Socinus. It would be idle to suppose it dormant in an age of intellectual restlessness like the present. It would be dangerous to feel confident that it is not working in ourselves. The form which it most commonly assumes now, under the action of the prevalent current of metaphysical opinion, is the tenet, more or less distinctly held, that man, the αὐτὸς ἐγώ, or individual self, is the measure of truth and falsehood. It is a natural reaction, perhaps, from the long dominion of the philosophy of mere sensation, that the intuitions of the human intellect, which that had overlaid, if not denied altogether, should be brought out into a prominence and invested with a significance, which equally destroy, in their turn, the balance of nature and truth. So it is, however, that we are taught now,—and multitudes more or less consciously are being moulded by the teaching,—that in these intuitions lie the criteria of truth and falsehood, right and wrong; that the laws of immutable morality are graven upon the human heart; and that conscience, instead of merely a judge who passes sentence upon actions according to their conformity with an imperfect internal and a perfect revealed law, has in herself the law by which all outward revelation must be judged. Our moral convictions, indeed, are held to be as unquestionable truth, as are our intellectual axioms: they are our nature, part of the unchangeable system of the universe. By them, therefore, all outward moral agencies must be measured. Not only human laws; not merely the acts and sentiments and characters of other men; but all that purports to reveal to us God and His dealings and His will, must be tried by this standard; and, by their conformity or disagreement with it, must be accepted as right, or rejected as wrong. No strength of external evidence can support a revelation, or any part of it, which this internal tribunal condemns. Historic truth is only probability; the intuitions of the moral faculty are absolute certainty. Human testimony however strong, the apparent verdict of the senses however clear, are but contingent and fallible; and cannot prevail against what is *felt* to be true or false, right or wrong.

Holy Scripture, therefore, on this theory, can be a rule of faith, only when it has been tried and gauged by the inner and supreme rule of our own consciousness, and only so far forth as it agrees with it. By this we rightly, and even necessarily, judge of both the form and the matter of what professes to be a revelation,—of the casket and of the treasure it contains. The books of the Bible are genuine and authentic, not in proportion as they are sustained by external testimony, but in proportion as they commend themselves as such to the critic mind. Style is a better evidence than the consent of antiquity, and the turn of a phrase than the quotation of a contemporary. An Apostle could not have written, what we feel he ought not to have written; and paragraphs and epistles must be rejected, if they do not seem to harmonise with other passages, or with our ideas of the character or circumstances of the writer. Narrative, however well attested, must be subjected to the searching criticism of the judgment. All that is miraculous must be at once eliminated,—supported, as it is, only by external testimony, but contradicted by the inner sense. The test must be applied unsparingly. Discrepancies are confessions of falsehood; coincidences are to be suspected of art. What we think men would have done, is more probable than what we are told they did; and the assertions of the writer are as a feather in the balance against the intuitions of the reader.

Exposed to such a process, the history of the Bible, like every other history in the world, crumbles away. It matters not. The great doctrines revealed stand, it is said, on a firmer foundation than the outward circumstances of revelation could supply. These are, in fact, for the most part but accretions round the doctrine, the deposit of human credulity and superstition; myths, which, in all ages, have a tendency to group themselves and crystallise about a central truth. But, then, the doctrines themselves must be brought to the same tribunal; and can be received as coming from God, so far only as they tally with the peculiarities of our moral nature, satisfy the cravings of the soul, and chime in harmony with our intuitions of truth and falsehood, right and wrong. And the results of this investigation must be followed, even should they lead us to throw off, one by one, all the peculiar and (as we once thought) heart-stirring doctrines of the Gospel, and even all definite tenets of Deism; and should leave us pondering on the almost verbal question, whether there be any God, or whether all is god, and we and all things but portions of the circumambient Deity.

I have sketched this prevalent form of intellectual pride in its tendencies; tendencies, however, which have been realised, and by minds of no ordinary strength and temper. But more usually they are but partially developed; and in this stage may remain within the Church, and sap and pervert, without destroying, the faith and comfort of Christians. Thus held, they tend to weaken and underrate the external evidences of Christianity, and, at the breaches made by a self-confident criticism, let in a thousand doubts and difficulties, which shake the soul and disturb its vision of things unseen and spiritual. Men explain away, without formally rejecting, doctrines, which are offences to others and difficulties to themselves: and envelope the clear and (as they feel) harsh outline of revealed truth in a cloud of ingenious commentary, which leaves much of the language of the Gospel without a meaning, and all its morality without a motive. In this way, some who are still believers, hold in suspense, as a kind of open question, the miraculous evidences of Christianity (the only foundation of a vigorous faith); and their minds, being in unstable equilibrium, are incapable of doing or suffering any thing great or good for the Gospel's sake: while others surrender, one by one, to the demands of the intuitive philosophy, the tenets of the Trinity, the atonement, the resurrection, the judgment, and eternal punishment, as the Church Catholic has learnt them from the pages of Scripture; contenting themselves with the name and shadow of truths, from which the reality and power are gone.

It belongs not to this time and place to trace these streams of error up to their sources, amidst the heights of the cloudy metaphysics whence they sprung: nor am I concerned at present to show, how the system which results involves its own refutation, in the innumerable contradictions between the conclusions of those who yet appeal to the same inward and immutable standard, and in the impossibility, oftentimes, of granting the postulates of its teachers,—the existence, for example, of feelings and cravings in one's own mind, which it is asserted we must have, but which in all sober sincerity we are sure we have not.

I am addressing myself to those who believe the Scriptures to be the word of God, but who are necessarily exposed to the contagion of this mental habit in its prevalent type, entering as it does largely into much of the popular literature, and even theology of the day: and I would desire, by way of warning, to lay the system side by side with that of the Gospel, in order that, should they appear irreconcileably at variance, we may at least know beforehand the direction in which it tends, and not, by supposing it to be the same, or parallel, with that of revelation, be led by it imperceptibly to error, scepticism, or infidelity.

Now in order to constitute self, either in its intentions or reasoning processes, the criterion of truth and falsehood, right and wrong, it must be assumed either that human nature has of itself this faculty of moral discernment, or that, not having it of itself, it is, at least, in virtue of the Gospel, universally gifted with it. According to the one hypothesis, there is woven in the original texture of our moral constitution a critical faculty, whose verdicts are authoritative and decisive. According to the other, though it be admitted that the intrinsic moral judgment was injured by original sin and its consequences, there is a supernatural illumination granted to all, or at least all who realise and use it; spiritual influence, coextensive with man's need, is peculiar to no one dispensation, nor the privilege of any particular creed; inspiration is the same in its source and kind, whether its result be what is noble in the strains of Homer, what is good in the maxims of Confucius or the teaching of Socrates, what is true in the discoveries of Newton and Laplace, what is revealed in the writings of Isaiah and of Paul, or what is felt in the intuitions of each one who is in earnest to know what is right; consequently, there is in all an extrinsic power of judging, with which even what appears to be taught in the records of revelation, must coincide, if true, and to whose dictates we are bound to listen, lest we should neglect the Spirit of God.

To turn now to the pages of the Gospel; and, for greater conciseness, to one passage, in which the very point,—the power of the discernment of revealed truth,—is under discussion, the two opening chapters of the Epistle from which I have taken my text. The Apostle had been led to dwell on the character of his ministry at Corinth. He there proclaimed the broad facts and fundamental truths of the Gospel, without the embellishments of human eloquence or the refinements of human wisdom. "He preached Christ crucified." Thus taught, the truth was rejected by those whom the world would think best qualified to judge. "Not many wise men after the flesh, not many mighty, not many noble, were called. But God chose the foolish things of the world to confound the wise, and weak things of the world to confound the mighty." God, not the critical faculty of the hearers, was the discriminating agent by whom the Apostle's auditors were grouped into two classes; those to whom the Gospel was a "stumbling-block" or "foolishness," and those to whom it was "Christ, the power of God and the wisdom of God." And that it might appear to be God, and neither the preacher's nor the hearer's wisdom, was one purpose of the mode of teaching adopted. "My speech and my preaching was not with enticing words of man's wisdom, but in demonstration of the Spirit and of power: that your faith should not stand in the wisdom of men, but in the power of God."

More specifically, in the sequel, this divine agent, by whom both Paul spoke and his converts believed, is defined to be the Holy Spirit, God the Holy Ghost. We, apostles, too, he continues, foolish as we are deemed, speak wisdom among the perfect; wisdom, however, not of this world nor of the leading men of this world who are coming to nought, but we speak God's wisdom in a mystery, revealing that which was hidden, which no one of the leading men of this world knew. But *to us*, he continues, after illustrating his position by a reference to Isaiah, God has revealed them by His Spirit. For the Spirit searcheth and knoweth all things, even the deep things of God. For (to employ an analogy which, though, if followed in other directions, it would lead to serious error, is exactly here in point), in the case of men, who knows the things of a man save the spirit of man which is in him? so also the things of God no one knows save the Spirit of God. By Him, therefore, and Him alone, the preacher teaches, and the hearer believes. We, apostles, have not received the spirit of the world, but the Spirit which is from God, that we may know the things freely imparted to us by God; which we speak, too, in words not taught by human wisdom, but by the Spirit, expressing the teaching of the Spirit in the language of the Spirit. And as to the hearers,—the unspiritual man, ψυχικὸς ἄνθρωπος,—man in the completeness of his own nature, and, therefore, capable of the highest degrees of the wisdom of this world, but without the Spirit,—the unspiritual man does not receive the things of the Spirit of God, for they are foolishness to him (as the preaching of Christ crucified was to the Greek philosophers), and he is not able to know them, because they are judged of spiritually. But the spiritual man,—he who has the Spirit,—judges of all things, but he himself is judged of by no one. For who (again to enforce the truth by a passage from Isaiah) knows the mind of Jehovah, who shall instruct him? what unaided *man*, that is, knows the things of God? But *we*, who are spiritual, being taught by the Spirit of Christ, have the mind of Christ.

1. It results from this passage, first, that, according to the scheme of Christianity, the critical faculty, —the power of judging of the truth and falsehood, the good and evil of revelation,—is external to man; no constituent part of his moral constitution, but an extrinsic power, working in and with his own faculties doubtless, but still distinct from himself, and given him by God. The spirit of the man knows only the things of the man; the things of God are known only by the Spirit of God; and are only spiritually judged of.

2. It follows too, secondly, that the gift of this extrinsic power is not universal. It was in explanation of the fact that his gospel had been rejected by so many both of Jews and Greeks, that the Apostle stated the doctrine, that the unspiritual man does not receive the things of the Spirit of God. The ψυχικοὶ, who had not the Spirit, were co-extensive, then, with those who heard but were not converted; probably, at that time, as ever, the large majority: while they who could judge of all things, were still the Saviour's little flock.

3. And, thirdly we infer, that this gift is not the

same in kind (though doubtless, as every good gift, it may be traced up at last to the same source, the Father of lights) with that which exists as wisdom, foresight, genius, and other intellectual endowments, in the noble and great of this world. Not many such hearers were called, when the Apostle preached. They remained, for the most part, unspiritual, and incapable of receiving or judging of the things of the Spirit of God: while the gift was given to those who believed, though humble in intellect, acquirements, and station. " God chose the foolish things of the world to confound the wise, and the weak things of the world to confound the things which are mighty."

It does not, indeed, follow from the Apostle's words, that God, in bestowing the gift of spiritual discernment, does not require the co-operation of the human will; nor again, that the Holy Spirit, though itself the illuminating Agent, does not work with, in, and by the faculties of the human intellect. All this must be admitted, and indeed maintained, in spite of metaphysical difficulties which we are incapable of solving. But it does, I think, follow, that according to the teaching of Holy Scripture, so far from man's intuitions, or consciousness, or self in any form, being the judge of truth and falsehood, right and wrong, (as far, at any rate, as truth and right are the subjects of revelation) man himself, however high his mere intellectual endowments, is altogether incompetent to judge of them; the faculty of judging is an energy and gift of God the Holy Ghost; and it is not given to *all*, either as members of the human race, or as being within the visible pale of the Christian covenant, but, like all other gifts of the Spirit, as God wills, and, ordinarily, on the fulfilment of certain conditions and in the use of certain means.

And this leads to one or two practical remarks : for I am speaking to those, who,—whatever may be the interest and utility of studies and pursuits which call out the healthy play of intellect, and abundantly repay the toil they require by the treasures of æsthetic beauty and scientific truth,—are far more deeply interested, by their souls' innermost wants here and the awful problem of eternity, to know what is morally good and true and beautiful,—what God has taught, and what they are to believe and do. Then let me repeat, as resulting from the subject before us, the lesson, which, perhaps, is more often enforced than any other from this place,—but which can hardly be enforced too often,—that the first condition for the appreciation of revealed truth are habits of purity, humility and self-restraint. The faculty which appreciates is heaven-descended, the gift of the Holy Spirit: and the Holy Spirit dwells not in the selfish, proud, or impure heart. Where thoughts of sin are readily entertained, or wilfully, even though timidly, dallied with; where there is an inner world of cherished day-dreams in which vanity enacts its own triumphs and revels in praise and honour of its own imagining; where self-indulgent ease or wilfulness follow their own ways with no felt and sustained exertion for God and others; there dwells not the Holy Spirit of God: or if His energy be yet striving there, those unheeded, ineffectual pleadings serve only to condemn. The eye of such a soul is dim to spiritual truth. It cannot discern the colours of right and wrong. It is but the perception of the natural man, eminent though it may be for this world's wisdom: and "the natural man receiveth not the things of the Spirit of God: for they are foolishness unto him: neither can he know them, because they are spiritually discerned." But when habits of increasing purity and holiness are at once the condition and the witness of the Spirit's presence, there the faculty of spiritual discernment,—which is the Spirit's gift,—finds its congenial soil and aliment: and he, whose initiation into the Christian mysteries is an humble and self-denying life, may hope to be admitted among those who "by reason of use have their senses exercised to discern both good and evil."[1]

Another inference I would draw, is the great importance, as an element of the study of revelation, of fervent prayer. Were the faculties of the natural man competent to the discrimination of revealed truth, we should even then do well to implore a blessing on their exercise, as we do before our ordinary business, or before our meals. But if the spiritual

[1] Heb. v. 14.

man alone judgeth all things; if without the light which is given from above the human soul is incompetent to discern the things of God; and if the Holy Spirit is promised and given by our heavenly Father to them that ask Him; then does prayer become, not merely the fitting adjunct, but the very soul and vivifying element of theological study, without which we have no reason, and no right, to expect to arrive at the truth. A very obvious inference this, brethren; but I fear a very needful one. I judge no one, but myself: but let each man's conscience reply, whether in the reading of the Holy Scriptures and in such studies as help to the knowledge of the same, his eye is often turned, as it should be, heavenward, and his heart raised towards the fount of all spiritual light, for grace to know, and power to do the truth. And maybe, he may find in that reply the solution of the difficulty, why his mind has been distracted often and wearied by doubts and wearing suspicions; or has been coldly conversant with the highest and most ennobling truths without kindling into emotion or thrilling with the pulse of hope: and he may learn to prize and practise, as the heaven-taught secret of all successful study, the precept of St. James: "If any of you lack wisdom, let him ask of God, that giveth to all men liberally and upbraideth not; and it shall be given him."[1]

Lastly, let us watch and check the growth of that

[1] James, i. 5.

intellectual habit (a form, or at least a product, of intellectual pride), which tends to erect itself into the standard of truth and falsehood, right and wrong. False as, I believe, it may be proved to be in philosophy, (though formed, doubtless, as are all other false theories, and exaggerated, on the nucleus of a neglected truth) it is irreconcileable, we have endeavoured to show, with the system which Paul taught and the early Christians believed. It cannot consist with the doctrine of a personal and specific agency of the Holy Spirit enabling to discern spiritual things, and guiding into the whole truth; and it is at variance, therefore, with that distrust of self, and that humble reliance on divine illumination and direction, which are traits in the childlike character to be found in all who enter into the kingdom of heaven. Prompting to an undue reliance on human strength which is weakness, and on human wisdom which God's word pronounces folly, and soon coming into collision with the plain teaching of Scripture and the doctrines which the universal Church has thence drawn, it results only too readily in paradox, uncertainty, error, heresy, or unbelief: and if it stops short of the last and worst of these, this is due often to the refusal of the heart, still clinging to holy associations and truths once felt to be true, to follow logical deductions to their dreary issue. Looking for our rule to God's word, proved to be His word by its external evidences echoed by its internal verisimilitude; acknowledging that for the due appreciation of this rule, and for its application to the discernment of what is good and true, we need the teaching of the Holy Spirit; earnestly seeking His promised aid, and humbly trusting to it, as we endeavour to know and do God's will; we are safe. He will guide us into all needful truth. But to desert this "anchor of the soul sure and steadfast," and to steer our course in a proud independence, by the indications of our intuitions or our unaided judgment, is to drift onward towards a godless philosophy, whose truths are that which each one troweth, and whose morality, that which each one listeth.

SERMON XI.

SELF-CONCEIT ITS OWN PUNISHMENT.

ROMANS, xii. pt. 16.

Be not wise in your own conceits.

IT is a peculiar excellence of God's moral government, that, as far as it is carried out in this life, its laws vindicate themselves. They need no executive external to their own sanctions; but each violation of their dictates carries in itself the germ of its own punishment, slowly, perhaps, but surely to be developed in its season. And though it is more astonishing, and more suited, therefore, for some of the divine purposes, when the arm of God is bared, as it were, and, as in the Jewish economy, openly distributes the rewards and penalties which in general silently follow the conduct to which they respectively belong; yet are His wisdom, justice, and holiness still more apparent, when His violated laws are found to be their own stern avengers; and when it results naturally from those links of cause and effect which science generalizes into the principles of political philosophy, political economy, or medicine, that injustice begets civil discord, extravagance is punished by poverty, intemperance is followed by disease, and an old age of peevish imbecility is the penalty of a licentious youth.

But though this peculiarity of the Divine government may be traced in the political and physical consequences which result from transgressions of its laws, it is, perhaps, more striking in their moral effects. In the history of the human heart, every fault, for the most part, enfolds its own punishment, and inflicts it usually on that very part of the inner man which erred; disappointing the desire, or mortifying the appetites, which were the first movers towards the transgression; so that it is not so certain that the Egyptians were punished by the objects of their own depraved worship and their deities became their plagues, as it is that most vices prevaricate with the desires they profess to gratify, and while they present them with a shadowy and guilty fruition, blast those real and innocent enjoyments which God intended for them. The voluptuary seeks pleasure, but finds satiety and disgust: in moderation and the healthful exercise of his faculties he would have attained the object of his search. The covetous man never reaches the *enough* he covets; but which charitable industry has, and is thankful for. The envious is tormented that his success is less than that of another; and thus infuses tenfold bitterness in a bitter cup. In every instance, our well-being is bound up with our well-doing; and God commands us to be happy, when He commands us to be holy.

But obvious as this is in the case of many vices, it is not, perhaps, sufficiently borne in mind, how close is its application to the class of sins forbidden in the words of the text, " Be not wise in your own conceits." Undue self-esteem, comprising the various forms and degrees of conceit, affectation, vanity, pride, and ambition, is the abuse of a natural and useful element of our moral constitution,—the complacency which we feel towards anything good in ourselves, either discovered by consciousness, or indicated by the approbation of others. The purpose of this faculty is to urge us on in the pursuit of excellence, and its end is the true dignity of our nature. As such, it is nowhere condemned in Scripture; but rather appealed to as a motive, and pointed to its proper objects. " Whatsoever things are lovely, whatsoever things are of good report; if there be any virtue, and if there be any praise," Christians are to " think on these things."[1] There is an " honour that cometh from God,"[2] as well as the praise of men. And the Apostle writes to the Galatians, contrasting this moral faculty with its abuse, " If any man think himself to be something when he is nothing, he deceiveth himself. But let every man prove his own work, and then shall he have rejoicing in himself alone, and not in another."[3]

[1] Phil. iv. 8.   [2] John, v. 44; Rom. ii. 29.
[3] Gal. vi. 3, 4

But, perhaps, no moral faculty has been so dislocated and warped by the fall of man as this; and none is so frequently or so variously abused. It is exerted on wrong objects and in undue degrees. It becomes *the* motive instead of *a* motive of action. It swells, and usurps, and feeds on thoughts of its own originating, till self becomes everything, and God and duty nothing. It is sinful, and the fruitful parent of innumerable sins. But it is not of the sinfulness of self-conceit (to use one word for the class) of which I wish to speak; but of the way in which, according to the usual procedure of God's moral government, it defeats its own ends, and thus works its own punishment. It is an undue appreciation of our own real or imagined excellences and a mistaken pursuit of dignity and honour: but it is, at the same time, a hindrance to intellectual, and a bar to moral and religious excellence; while it fails entirely of its end, —the true dignity of human nature.

1. To be wise in our own conceit is a hindrance to intellectual excellence, though it is not a bar to it. Undue estimation of self,—pride, vanity, even conceit,—frequently accompany great mental powers, and may even be the spur and motive to their exercise: and too often the admiration with which we view intellectual greatness, is changed into a smile of pity akin to contempt by the moral littleness of him who is endowed with it. But though compatible with a high degree of intellectual ex-

cellence, there is no doubt that this vice is a hindrance to the highest; that those who are great in spite of it, would be much greater without it; and that the cumbrous garb of vanity and conceit confines and stunts, though it cannot fetter, the movements of a powerful mind.

1. And this on many accounts. Self-conceit, for example, prejudices the mind against truth. Men usually take up opinions first, and examine them afterwards. Most men commit themselves by the utterance of such opinions before they have examined them. Indeed, it is often only by the conflict with the opinions of others, and the shock of repulsion from the world without, that we are forced to consider the grounds of our belief, and to test the strength of its foundations. Now the humble mind can do this impartially, content to be corrected, and willing to give up whatever will not bear the trial of a careful investigation. But self-conceit is pledged to an opinion once expressed. It cannot give it up without inflicting on itself a wound from which it shrinks. It has a deep interest in determining the question in conformity with preconceived notions. And, therefore, all the elements of proof and the antecedents of the reasoning process which should determine it, are viewed through a medium of prejudice, and deflected from the right line. The result is often falsehood, obstinately maintained as truth. It is difficult to calculate how large an amount of heresy in religion

and error in science may be traced to opinions, first rashly uttered, then defended under the influence of a false shame, at length believed, loved, and propagated.

2. Again, undue self-esteem hinders in the search of truth by leading us to reject useful helps. It makes us confident in the powers of self, and unwilling to be indebted to others. It values the credit of a discovery, more than the possession of a truth; and it learns the success of other men's investigations, rather with disappointment that its hope of distinction has been lost, than with satisfaction that a step in knowledge has been gained.

3. Nor is our choice of subjects of study uninfluenced by this leaven of the whole inner man. Almost unconsciously we are led to the more showy instead of the more real; the pebbles glittering on the surface, instead of the gold imbedded in the mine. Any question, however empty, provided men's eyes are upon it; any logomachy, however vain, provided the contest is raging; will attract the mental powers which vanity wields, more than the patient investigation of truths not yet in dispute, though they involve men's best interests and the honour of God. And many a weary trifler, whose vanity has perverted noble powers to unworthy purposes, has confessed with one who had far less reason than themselves, "Vitam perdidi, operosè nihil agendo."

4. But there is another effect of self-conceit on the intellect, less obvious, perhaps, but well deserving the consideration of all, and especially of the young student; I mean its tendency to dissipate the attention and to weaken the power of concentrating the mind. I need not say here, that, great as are the differences of mental endowments between man and man, yet even more than on original talent does intellectual eminence depend on the faculty, natural or acquired, of concentrating the attention on the subject before us. Without this the finest abilities are wasted in desultory and profitless efforts. There may be the light and heat; but the lens is wanting to gather them into the luminous point, which alone can fuse the mingled mass, and disengage from error the pure residuum of truth. Now this intellectual faculty, no less than most moral virtues, requires in some sort a negation of self. The mind cannot think on two things at once. It passes from one to the other, and its tension is weakened by the transit. Its eye, like the body's eye, carries with it a spectrum of that on which it has been gazing, which dims the object to which it turns. But some such spectrum is always present in the vain man's mind. Self is ever flitting before him. His reputation and prospects; what others will think or say of him; how he can turn the knowledge he is acquiring, into the coin of reputation and praise; these thoughts are constantly mingling with his studies, distracting his attention, and re-

laxing the hold of his mental powers, and often breaking the chain of reasoning, or obliterating some idea just traced upon the page of memory. With many, such thoughts are allowed to expand into day-dreams of vanity or ambition, in which the dreamer enacts scenes of fancied success, and exults as the hero of imagined triumphs, while the instruments, perhaps, by the patient use of which alone success can be attained, are lying forgotten before him. And there are men, who have indulged in this mental opium (so to speak), till they are not only less fitted but incapacitated for exertion; who live in a world of their own, peopled with their own praises, till their flaccid powers and sensitive imaginations are quite unable to cope with the realities of the hard, unadmiring world without, and they retire into themselves, —men who might have been useful and happy, but for vanity,—to loiter away life in a peevish, self-idolising misanthropy.

But enough has been said to show, how to be wise in our own conceit becomes, in some degree at least, a hindrance to intellectual excellence, and thus involves a self-inflicted punishment; stunting the merits of which it covets the reward; unnerving for the contest of which it hopes the crown.

II. But it is more important to observe, that such undue estimation of self is not merely a hindrance, but a bar, to moral and religious excellence; that it destroys true virtue, and is incompatible with holiness; and that, therefore, it is not a foible merely, nor a folly, but a sin.

1. For, first, it corrodes at once the very root of all goodness by vitiating the motives of action. It is admitted that the motives from which even the best men act are mixed; and we have stated self-approbation and complacency in what is right to be a principle of our nature, intended to actuate us, and, therefore, to actuate us, doubtless, in the choice and pursuit of what is morally good: but it is one motive out of many; not the highest, and never meant to be the sole or the chief. The reverence and love of God, gratitude to the Redeemer who has bought us with His own blood, and the approbation of right because it is right, should combine to form a complex sense of duty, constraining us to do what is good, irrespective of its consequences. If the praise of men results, we may accept it: if it does not, we may well be content without it. It was not this for the sake of which we acted. But the man wise in his own conceits, *does* act for this end. Self has taken the place of God and duty. The desire of admiration, praise, or aggrandizement is the spring which moves him. And, therefore, whatever may be his efforts or successes; though he may be an example to others and a benefactor of mankind; "though he bestow all his goods to feed the poor, and give his body to be burned;" yet, as obedience in the sight of God, or even as virtue tried by the rules of sound morality, all is vitiated by the

Self-conceit its own Punishment.

poor, mean, selfish motive. "Either make the tree good, and his fruit good; or else make the tree corrupt, and his fruit corrupt."[1]

2. But even where other and better motives are not excluded, self-conceit has a tendency to dwarf all singleness of purpose, and, consequently, to slacken energy of character. A great and good man is one who sets a good object before him, and pursues it with steady unwavering resolution. It is his one main purpose, and all his faculties are concentrated on it. But the vain man, if seeking God's glory and man's good at all, is at the same time seeking his own reputation. The two ends are never identical, often opposed. He has, then, to choose between the two; that is, either to mortify his vanity, or to do what he knows to be wrong: or, as is usually the case, to endeavour to reconcile them by some miserable compromise, unable to act effectually because unprepared to act boldly, and losing both ends by trying to grasp them both. "A double-minded man is unstable in all his ways."[2]

3. But to look deeper; the spirit of which we are speaking, palsies the very life of religion, because it deadens prayer and distracts the feelings of devotion. Busy at all times as are thoughts of vanity, they are never more busy than when we are on our knees. I state the fact, I do not explain it. It will suggest its own explanation to those who believe, that "we

[1] Matt. xii. 33.   [2] James, i. 8.

wrestle," in this life's battle-field, "not against flesh and blood, but against principalities, against powers, against the rulers of the darkness of this world, against spiritual wickedness in high places."[1] But where vain thoughts have been indulged, and have gathered into a habit of self-conceit, they are ever obtruding themselves on our devotions. They flit between the soul and God. They catch the upturned gaze of prayer, and lure it to follow some pageant of fancy's painting, till the soul wakes suddenly from its dream, and finds that the lips have been praying without it, and that it has been mocking God with an unreal semblance of worship. Nor can anything master them, but a habit of unfeigned humility, formed by the teaching of the Holy Spirit. Nothing external can. They go with us to the most sacred places, and are scarcely checked by the most solemn scenes. Vain thoughts flutter in the vain heart, in God's Church, on the steps of the altar, by the bed of the dying, and on the brink of the open grave. And where they are, how can that clogged, wandering prayer, scarce issuing from the occupied breast, rise upwards to the throne of grace, or find from a holy and jealous God acceptance and a blessing?

4. To be wise in our own conceit must also be incompatible with true penitence; not, indeed, with sorrow for particular sins, nor even with the bitterest

[1] Eph. vi. 12.

remorse, when the unrenewed heart will sometimes make amends, as it were, for its own sufferings by priding itself upon them, and can even find a strange delight in anatomizing its own moral maladies before the eyes of others, to be repaid by their sympathy and astonishment. But it is inconsistent with the broken and contrite heart of true penitence, the very staple of which is a deep sense of unworthiness. The soul, convinced of sin by the Holy Ghost, finds nothing left on which to pride itself. Its language, as it looks up to its wronged Maker and Redeemer, is, " Behold, I am vile ; what shall I answer thee ? I will lay mine hand upon my mouth."[1] It does not plead anything of its own, not even its own sincerity. It is thoroughly humbled. And in the truth that vanity and true penitence cannot exist together, lies much of the force of our Saviour's solemn warning, " Except ye be converted, and become as little children, ye shall not enter into the kingdom of heaven."[2]

5. Again, self-conceit in its various forms is a hindrance to faith. " How can ye believe," asked our Lord, " which receive honour one of another, and seek not the honour that cometh from God only?"[3] We have already seen, how undue self-esteem hinders the search and attainment of truth by prejudicing the judgment, neglecting the useful assistance of others, and leading to what is new and striking, rather than to what is true. But besides these influ-

[1] Job, xl. 4. [2] Matt. xviii. 3. [3] John, v. 44.

ences, which operate in their fullest force on inquiries into religious truth in general, the man " wise in his own conceit" is peculiarly ill-fitted to judge candidly of the truth and doctrines of the revelation of the Gospel. He is prejudiced against it as such. The very necessity of a revelation humbles the pride of intellect. It implies that there are bounds to its powers, and limits to its domain. It convicts it of ignorance. It brings to check the mind that has detected the component atoms of matter, and counted the vibrations of the sunbeam, and measured the orbs of heaven, and says to it, even when approaching the highest and noblest objects of contemplation, " Hitherto shalt thou come, but no further." And the prejudice is strengthened, when revelation is found to contain mysteries. The vain mind chafes at mysteries,—truths which it cannot grasp, cannot analyze; and which it must receive, if it receives them at all, as a child believes a parent's words which it cannot understand.

But besides the offences which it throws in the way of intellectual pride, the Gospel is peculiarly distasteful to self-conceit on account of the humiliating conditions of the salvation it reveals. To struggle sternly with evil, trampling every appetite under the overmastering will, and subjecting all external circumstances to the mind's control; to meditate on the good and beautiful and infinite, till the soul, sublimed from earth and earthly things, is assimilated to what

Self-conceit its own Punishment. 197

she contemplates, and prepared, when the ties which bind her to the body are severed, to mingle with the essence of the deity ; even to macerate or mangle the body by self-inflicted austerities, and to purchase future happiness by the intensity of present suffering ;—all this the pride of man is ready to accept. But to be saved wholly by the sufferings and merits of another; to be indebted for God's pardon, favour, promises of glory, to a righteousness which is not our own, and an atonement which we did not make ourselves ; to lie low at the foot of the cross with no worthiness but the feeling of our unworthiness, no claim but that of mercy for another's sake ; to acknowledge that all we have of good is wrought in us, not by us ; that the holiest saint is but God's workmanship who has nothing which he has not received ; —such truths fall coldly on the vain and swelling heart. They are " hard sayings." He would not have them true. And the Gospel is rejected altogether on some pretence, which would never satisfy any but those who were anxious to be satisfied ; or assented to with that uninterested acquiescence, which has little in common, but the misapplied name, with a hearty, living, actuating faith.

6. But I must hasten to the solemn truth, which, most of all, makes vanity and self-conceit a bar to moral and religious excellence ; and which lies, indeed, at the root of all that has hitherto been said. These habits are not compatible with the effectual grace of

the Holy Spirit. He, the seal of God's people, the earnest of their inheritance, and the source of all holiness, abides not in the vain heart. "For thus saith the high and lofty One that inhabiteth eternity, whose name is Holy; I dwell in the high and holy place, with him also that is of a contrite and humble spirit, to revive the spirit of the humble, and to revive the heart of the contrite ones."[1] "Though the Lord be high, yet hath he respect unto the lowly: but the proud he knoweth afar off."[2] "God resisteth the proud, and giveth grace to the humble."[3] It is not the grosser sins merely that desecrate the temple, which at baptism was consecrated to be God's,—the pollutions of the flesh, the world's covetousness, malice and envy and indulged thoughts of impurity; —but pride and vanity setting up the idol self there, and diverting to its service purposes and energies which belong to God. The Spirit is resisted, grieved, quenched. And as from Him alone proceeds every pure and holy motive, the single eye which leads straight on to great and good ends, earnestness of prayer and truthfulness of devotion, real, felt penitence, and the faith which justifies and works by love; it needs no more to show that those habits which cannot remain where the Spirit is, must ever be a bar by their presence to all that is excellent, and must destroy the substance, though they may leave the form, of virtue, religion, and holiness.

[1] Isaiah, lvii. 15.   [2] Ps. cxxxviii. 6.   [3] James, iv. 6.

III. One step further. To be wise in our own conceit not only defeats its own object by hindering or destroying the excellence for which it covets admiration and praise; but it fails entirely of its end, —the true dignity of human nature. I am not speaking here of its frequent failures in the pursuit of what is falsely thought dignity; nor of the certainty with which, in some of its forms, it is punished by the sneer of ridicule or the contemptuous smile of pity. But I mean, that it has totally mistaken its end. The true dignity of human nature is humility. Real greatness is the knowledge of our own real littleness. "Whosoever shall exalt himself, shall be abased; and he that shall humble himself shall be exalted." [1]

1. For, first, the humble Christian is like Christ, and like him in what is made, as it were, his distinguishing characteristic. "Rejoice greatly, O daughter of Zion," thus the prophet predicted His coming; "shout, O daughter of Jerusalem: behold thy King cometh unto thee: he is just and having salvation." And how shall He be known, this mighty Monarch? What are the ensigns of His sovereignty? "He is lowly and riding upon an ass, and upon a colt the foal of an ass." [2] His own character of Himself was that he was "meek and lowly of heart;" [3] and humility is called by St. Paul "the mind which was in Christ Jesus." [4] The humble, therefore, are

[1] Matt. xxiii. 12. [2] Zech. ix. 9.
[3] Matt. xi. 29. [4] Phil. ii. 5.

like him, and bear the badge of that high brotherhood. Conformed to His image, they become partakers of His glory; and even as His majesty shone most in His humility, so it is reflected in theirs. Made like the Lord from heaven in this His distinguishing attribute, their human nature is exalted above itself; and " beholding as in a glass the glory of the Lord, they are changed into the same image from glory to glory, even as by the Spirit of the Lord." [1]

2. Still more does the dignity of humility result from the union of true believers with Christ and God. The contrite and humble spirit is Jehovah's spiritual tabernacle; and it was to his "little children," to those who in humility had entered the kingdom of heaven and become the followers of Him who was meek and lowly of heart, that our Saviour said, "I will pray the Father, and he shall give you another Comforter, that he may abide with you for ever; even the Spirit of truth; whom the world cannot receive, because it seeth him not, neither knoweth him: but ye know him; for he dwelleth in you and shall be with you. I will not leave you comfortless; I will come to you. . . . If a man love me he will keep my words; and my Father will love him, and we will come unto him and make our abode with him." [2] Christians, where pride, or other sin, has not grieved the Spirit and provoked him to depart, are the temples of the Holy Ghost. It is a want of

[1] 2 Cor. iii. 18.   [2] John, xiv. 16—18, 23.

faith, then, or of consideration, which prevents us from realizing the dignity of true humility. For if these things be true, what have earthly honours to compare with them? We might be respected, esteemed, caressed; we might be noted by the finger of admiration, and lauded by the voice of fame; we might be the friends of the monarch or the favourites of the people; we might have reached the height of glory and the pinnacle of earthly grandeur;—yet surely to the eye of sober judgment, scanning invisible as well as visible things, it is nothing thus to be great amidst this world's littleness, compared with the dignity of Him in whom the world's Creator vouchsafes to dwell, the chosen habitation of "the high and lofty One that inhabiteth eternity." Surely to be one with Christ in God, to be a member of Him who filleth all things, as much surpasses all this life's honours and relationships, as heaven transcends earth, —the everlasting future, the little span of our present existence.

3. From this union with Christ follows another feature in the dignity of the humble; that they represent Christ, and through Him, the Father, on earth; – stand, as it were, in Their place towards those who do them good or evil. "Whosoever shall receive this child in my name receiveth me, and whosoever shall receive me, receiveth him that sent me."[1] "But whoso shall offend one of these little ones which

[1] Luke, ix. 48.

believe in me, it were better for him that a millstone were hanged about his neck, and that he were drowned in the depth of the sea."[1] "Inasmuch as ye have done it unto one of the least of these my brethren, ye have done it unto me."[2] And if we count it high honour when one, an ambassador, represents the sovereign of some foreign kingdom, so that the respect due to his master is paid to him, and an insult offered to him, is resented as if offered to his prince; how much greater is their dignity who represent the King of kings and Lord of lords, and in whose persons *He* is benefited or wronged, whose throne is on the right hand of God "far above all principality and power and might and dominion and every name that is named, not only in this world, but also in that which is to come." Persecuted or loved, received or rejected, they are His, and in His stead. They represent Him on earth; and their credentials are humility.

4. And, lastly, the dignity of the humble consists in their future inheritance, the glory purchased and reserved for them hereafter. It is the habit of estimating actions and character, good and evil, by their reference only to this life, without taking into account their bearings on eternity, which makes our judgment so often at variance with the word of God. The humble disciples of our Lord, for instance,—those whom he designates His little children,—may often

[1] Matt. xviii. 6.   [2] Matt. xxv. 40.

be little esteemed here. With few, perhaps, of the qualities which the world admires; with much that it cannot appreciate or understand; lowly sometimes in station and tried by affliction, they are often, like their Master, " despised and rejected of men ;" ridiculed, maybe, and scoffed at by the ungodly, and even by others looked down upon with the pity which is allied to contempt. At the best, there is nothing in their condition *as Christians*, to gain honour or command admiration. But extend your view from this world to the next, beyond the few brief years which form the vestibule of eternity, and your estimate must be entirely changed. This corruptible has put on incorruption; this mortal has put on immortality. Sown in dishonour, they are raised in glory; sown in weakness, they are raised in power. They who have followed their Lord in His humiliation, are advanced to be with Him in His dignity. Conformed to Him in meekness now, when He appears in glory " they are like Him, for they see Him as He is."[1] Those whom men despised, are become those whom God delighteth to honour. The poor fishermen of Galilee sit on twelve thrones judging the twelve tribes of Israel; and on the meekest brows and lowliest heads are set the most brilliant and unfading crowns. True even here, it will be far more evidently true, when the light of eternity dispels the dimness of our present conceptions and unveils the

[1] 1 John, iii. 2.

true proportion of things, that "whosoever exalteth himself shall be abased; and he that humbleth himself shall be exalted."[1]

If, then, I am addressing any whose pulse beats high with the love of fame, and who thirst for the praise and admiration of their fellow-men,—let me warn you not to lose the reality of honour for its shadow. While such are your motives and ends, you are cramping the free energies of intellect and stifling the vitality of religion. You may be successful, and success itself will be disappointment; but truly great and good you cannot be. Measured by the scale of revealed truth, ambition degrades; and to be wise in our own conceits is folly. While seeking only, or chiefly, the praise of men, you are losing the praise which is from God. While exalting yourself, you are preparing your own abasement. Let me point you to a nobler object of ambition. "Seek first the kingdom of God and His righteousness."[2] Enter His service through the low door of humility; and take up the cross of Him who was "meek and lowly of heart," on which to mortify each swelling thought and vain imagination. Seek habitually God's glory before your own, till He is everything, and self nothing. Be thus clothed with humility, and your reward is great in heaven. You may, or you may not, receive the praise of men. It matters little. If you do not, you have one temptation the less. But you will have the

[1] Luke, xiv. 11.   [2] Matt. v. 33.

praise which cometh from God only. The whole dignity of Christian humility will be yours. You will be conformed to the image of Him "in whom dwelleth all the fulness of the Godhead bodily." With you will abide " the High and lofty One that inhabiteth eternity." You will be privileged to represent Christ on earth, " so that they who do good to you, do good to Him." And by God's grace, and for the merits of His dear Son, you will be raised hereafter, when this world's honours have perished with the world itself, to share with Him who redeemed you, "a far more exceeding and eternal weight of glory." " He that is least among you all, the same shall be great."[1]

[1] Luke, ix. 48.

SERMON XII.

THE DANGERS TO THE CLERGY OF A TIME OF CONTROVERSY.

Preached in St. Paul's Cathedral, at the Visitation of the Lord Bishop of London, November, 1850.

1 Tim. iv. pt. 16.
Take heed unto thyself, and unto the doctrine.

To say that the present are perilous times for the Church of Christ would only be to repeat the complaint which has been made with reason in every age, since the time that the disciples, " the number of" whose " names together were" but " about one hundred and fifty," first met in the upper room at Jerusalem. It is, in fact, but to express in other words the truth, that Christ's people are still a little flock in a hostile world; and that Satan has never ceased to oppose the Church by open violence or more dangerous guile.

It might not even be correct to say that our times are more perilous than others. It is difficult to estimate the comparative danger of evils which differ in kind. There may often be more to fear, where less is feared. The lethargy may be as fatal as the fever: and the inner life of the Church may be decaying more surely, when no pain is felt nor disease suspected, than when the whole frame is racked by controversy or torn by schism.

It will, perhaps, be nearer the truth to say, that our days have their *peculiar* evils, which, like all evils, when present, seem to be worse than others to those who feel them. They have also, therefore, their peculiar dangers,—dangers to the Church at large; and dangers to its individual members, especially to those who administer the word and sacraments. These dangers it is our wisdom to estimate, guard against, and as much as possible to avoid. It might not, then, be unprofitable to survey them under any of these aspects: but on the present occasion I will confine myself to the consideration of some peculiar dangers which seem at this time to lie around the clergy,—the dangers to Christ's ministers of a time of controversy. And if, in so doing, I should seem to use words of censure,—who of all men have least right to do so,—bear in mind, Reverend brethren, that our own experience is, for the most part, the record, from which we must draw our descriptions of weakness, temptation, and peril; that we paint what we feel; and that the preacher, while addressing others, often is, and ought to be, pleading with himself. And to me, I confess, the discordant sounds of doubt, distrust, and controversy, which mar the harmony of our Church, seem all to blend into a solemn warning, speaking plainly to every minister of the Gospel of Jesus Christ, "Take heed unto thyself, and unto the doctrine."

The warning and the danger relate to *ourselves* in our ministerial capacity; or to the *doctrine* we teach.

I. 1. Of the dangers which encompass *ourselves* the most obvious is the loss of the grace of charity, the "most excellent" of the gifts of the Spirit, without which knowledge, eloquence, almsgiving, martyrdom, itself, is nothing. I call this a danger encompassing us as ministers, not because the laity are not exposed to it, for the charity of the whole body of Christ loses its warmth and tension during the fever of controversy,—but because we are more liable to suffer by it, in proportion as the subjects in dispute lie in the immediate range of our own duties, occupy more of our thoughts, and lie, perhaps, nearer to our hearts.

Nor should it be otherwise. God's truth should ever be the treasure, which God's minister should prize most dearly, and watch most jealously. But the difficult problem for frail and erring beings is, how to hold fast truth, when assailed, without breaking the links of charity and the bond of peace. It is easy, indeed, to say, that we are to love the erring while we hate his error, and to oppose his doctrine strenuously without holding him an enemy who teaches it. But to do this, requires unceasing watchfulness, a disciplined will, and the special aid of divine grace. Insensibly our feelings glide from an opinion to him who holds it. We are inclined to think worse of those who differ from ourselves. Opposition irritates. Prejudice and ill-will seat themselves in our breasts without alarming us, because we confound them with zeal for truth. We begin to hear others evil spoken of without displeasure, and, perhaps, to feel an emotion of joy at their misfortunes, or even their faults. And fallible men, to whom their brother's inmost heart is as a sealed book, dare to impute motives, to charge with consequences he never drew, and to throw about rashly the names of heresy and heretic; forgetting, that every error is not therefore heresy because we call it so, and that every one who holds a heresy, is not therefore a heretic.

And this danger would become greater, if, unhappily, rival associations should arise in our Church, formed for the defence of a principle, but becoming, almost necessarily, the nucleus of a party. It would ill become me to discuss the question, how far the adoption of such means for even the best ends implies a want of faith in the great Governor of the Church and in the vitality and powers of the government He has ordained; nor to inquire, whether to borrow from the world's politics an expedient, which has always been detrimental to the state, often the precursor of its downfall, can either expect or deserve a blessing. But this much must be allowed, that in

P

proportion as conflicting opinions and doctrines are respectively banded together by names and meetings and the tessera of membership, the infection of party spirit will be added to the other perils which surround us, and we shall have greater reason to "take heed to ourselves," lest, in the struggle for truth, we lose the priceless jewel of Christian charity.

2. Another danger of times of controversy is their tendency to withdraw us from our pastoral work. What a charge is laid upon us, brethren!—upon those especially, whose labour lies in the crowded districts of the metropolis and its suburbs, where a street might be a parish, and a pastor's day might well-nigh be spent in the swarming rooms of a single house. It is a task ever beginning, never ending; where the most untiring energy cannot overtake the duties to be done; and the weary labourer is often tempted to throw down his feeble tools, as he looks on the untilled portion of his Master's vineyard. Each day souls are passing into eternity, or drawing nearer to its unchangeable destinies, whom we were commissioned to warn, rebuke, instruct, or encourage; and whose blood, if they perish by our wilful negligence, will be required at our hands. Yet even the work of a parish priest, momentous as are its issues, and engrossing as should be its interest, palls by daily repetition. We are all too apt to weary of treading the same round, even though it be the race which God has set before us. Meanwhile come in

the stirring questions of the day,—important questions involving great truths, demanding and deserving our attention. And they obtain it. We are interested, excited, almost absorbed. To watch the progress of the controversy, to study the pleadings and balance the arguments, to take part, perhaps, in the van of the conflict, is an occupation which we are glad to consider a duty. It may be so. But we must be very careful, lest, in the mean time, the pastor's heart grows cold and his hands slack; lest our daily duties, which, because daily, are perhaps dull, are postponed or abridged; and lest our zeal for the Church and the Gospel draw us away by a specious pretext from the flock " over which the Holy Ghost hath made us overseers." And surely it would be success dearly purchased, if, while we were arguing successfully the cause of truth, one tempted soul have fallen, whom our visit might have upheld; one sinner have passed despairing to his account, whom we should have led to repentance and pointed to his Saviour.

3. Again; in times like these, we have reason to "take heed to ourselves," lest the spiritual tone of our mind and affections should be lowered. With this is closely united, not only the vigour of our own inner life, but much of our ministerial usefulness: and it is they only whose "affection is set on things above," and who " walk by faith not by sight," who, in the discharge of their high duty as Christ's ambas-

sadors, are "followers of Paul, even as he also was of Christ." But the spiritual mind is endangered by the struggle of controversy. I need not stay to point out, how surely the soul suffers, when the bonds of charity are broken, and ill-will and party rancour enter in at the breach which the discussion has made. The Holy Spirit is grieved, and His temple in the heart desecrated: and they only who " dwell in love, dwell in God and God in them." [1]

But this evil is obvious, and therefore, perhaps, less dangerous. There are others as real. For if the health of the spiritual life consists in a vivid perception of the truths of revelation, so that the thoughts dwell on them, the affections embrace them, and the preferences, purposes, and efforts of the man tend towards them as the great end and object of his being;—if, in short, it be to think, and feel, and live, as if God, and eternity, and heaven and hell, and the Saviour's love, and the Spirit's power, were *realities*, —the great realities of our existence;—it will follow, that whatever tends to weaken our perception of unseen truth, and to engross the thoughts and occupy the affections with other objects, does, so far, relax the energies and impair the well-being of the inner life of the soul. This, as we well know, is the danger of the world, over and above the positive sinfulness of many of its maxims and pursuits. But it is also the danger of religious controversy, even in defence

[1] 1 John, iv. 16.

of those very truths, which are the food of the life of faith. When the thoughts and feelings are occupied, not so much by the truths themselves, as by the defence of them; when it is the controversy, rather than the doctrine in question, in which we are interested; the very warmth of our zeal may tend to extinguish our piety. Faith is clogged by the panoply in which it fights. And men may argue for the Trinity, till their love for the triune God has grown cold; and defend the atonement, till the cross of Christ has well-nigh ceased to be a motive; support the doctrine of holy Baptism, till their keen sense is lost of the privileges and duties of a child of God; or dispute about the real presence, till the penitent faith is dulled, by which alone the body and blood of Christ are verily and indeed taken and received in the Lord's Supper. I say not that this need be, or that the risk of it may absolve those whose vow it is to banish and drive away all erroneous and strange doctrines, from their perilous duty. But I say that it *may* be; and that therefore, it concerns us all to "take heed to ourselves;" to watch and pray, lest the spiritual tone of our religion be lost or lowered, and the healthy glow of love and heavenward hope be faded by the breath and heat of controversy.

There is a light, indeed, under which times, like the present, may aid and invigorate the spiritual life; and under which we shall be wise to regard them. For as domestic affliction teaches us by a severe, but salutary, schooling that our home is not here, and draws our affections upward to a deathless family, gathering in the mansions of our Father's house; so should the scene which saddens us in the Church of Christ,—dissension where there should be unity, heart-burnings in the place of love, and doubts and errors marring our common faith,—feelingly convince us, that we are yet in the Church militant on earth, whose ranks are manned with fallible men, and whose enemies are openly opposing without, or plotting secretly within; and should raise our sad hearts to the Church triumphant in heaven, (our promise and inheritance,) "unto the city of the living God, the heavenly Jerusalem, and to an innumerable company of angels, to the general assembly and church of the firstborn which are written in heaven, and to God the judge of all, and to the spirits of just men made perfect, and to Jesus the mediator of the new covenant, and to the blood of sprinkling, that speaketh better things than that of Abel."[1] Thus our very temptations may strengthen our spiritual affections: and we may be saved from fruitless yearnings after what has not been promised here, a Church of perfect purity and holiness; and, perhaps, from erring to sects whose purity is but exclusiveness of profession, or to that Church, whose boasted unity is based on usurpation, and bound together by the despotic imposition of error.

[1] Heb. xii. 22-24.

II. But the text warns us to "take heed" not only "to ourselves" but "to our doctrine:" and there are dangers belonging to a time of controversy which may affect our teaching; and which, therefore, deserve the attention of those, whose duty it is "rightly to divide the word of truth."[1]

1. The main danger, perhaps, is a tendency to dwell on controverted points of doctrine, to the exclusion of, or at least in undue proportion to, the rest. We naturally crowd to the quarter where the citadel seems to be attacked, while the other battlements of our Zion may be left defenceless. And it is urged as a reason for insisting repeatedly on the same topic, that it is a truth which has been hitherto neglected, misunderstood, or disputed, and requires to be brought out, established, or enforced. To define it clearly, and to fix it conspicuously, may be the mission of the Church of our day. Add to this, that every man who is in earnest, is impelled, as it were, to speak to others of what has been interesting himself most deeply. "Out of the abundance of the heart the mouth speaketh."[2] And we would untie for our people the knots, either of doctrine or of conduct, which have most perplexed ourselves. And we are right. It *is* our duty to defend controverted truths, and to explain misunderstood or neglected doctrine; and the very secret of effective preaching is, that it be the transcript of the preacher's own con-

---

[1] 2 Tim. ii. 15.   [2] Matt. xii. 24.

victions and experience,— truths which he believes, arguments which have persuaded himself, trials and temptations which he has known, comforts which he has felt, hopes which he cherishes. The danger before us, then, lies in the line of duty: yet it is a danger notwithstanding. To teach any doctrine exclusively, or to give it undue prominence, is unprofitable to our people; is virtually erroneous teaching; and has a tendency to generate errors in an opposite direction.

It is unprofitable to our people: for it is by no means certain, that the error on which the controversies of the day are turning, is that to which they are most exposed; while it is quite certain, that they need instruction, as a body, on every point of Christian faith and practice; and that we must carefully lay the foundation of sound doctrine, as well as build upon it all the details of "instruction in righteousness." St. Paul took his hearers "to record" that he was "pure from the blood of all men," upon the ground, "that he had not shunned to declare unto them all the counsel of God."[1] But if our ordinary teaching dwells exclusively, or mainly, on one point, —however important we may think that point to be, —much must be left untaught, or taught imperfectly, which concerns the welfare of our people's souls.

But it deserves further to be considered, that to give any doctrine undue prominence is virtually erroneous teaching. Much error is partial truth. And

[1] Acts, xx. 26, 27.

though every portion of a revelation from God to man is true and precious, and cannot be neglected without sin; yet have the portions a relation and subordination one to another,—a relation and subordination which are part of the revelation itself; and which cannot be dislocated or neglected, without altering the units, as it were, of God's truth, and thus varying materially the sum total of Christian doctrine.

No one, for example,—though both are true— would place on the same level the doctrine of the atonement and that of the ministration of angels: and he who should dwell on the latter to the exclusion or neglect of the other, would be virtually preaching another gospel. So, too, to preach our Lord's divinity without His humanity, or His humanity without His divinity; justification by faith without the necessity of good works, or the necessity of good works without the need of divine grace; the atonement without the judgment, or the judgment without the atonement,—although every word spoken might be true, would be virtually and practically falsehood.

And even where other truths are not altogether omitted, yet to put in the fore-front of our teaching truths, which are subordinate or co-ordinate in Scripture; or by insisting too frequently on one topic to give it such importance in our hearers' minds that it overlaps and conceals the rest; is, in its degree, to mutilate the divine revelation, and, in effect at least, to inculcate or encourage error. We must be careful, then, while defending a doctrine, not to exaggerate its relative importance; nor in the warmth or demands of controversy to dwell so exclusively upon it, as to obscure in our people's conceptions and perhaps our own, truths equally necessary for our faith and practice.

Nor are we left without a standard and a guide: for we cannot but esteem it a peculiar happiness of our Church, and a cause of thankfulness to Him who has watched over her, that she has preserved in her formularies, not only the doctrines of the Gospel, but also the Scriptural proportion and analogy of faith, giving to each truth the prominence given to it in God's word, and linking them in the mutual dependence in which they have been revealed. She does not, for example, as others have done, lay down as the foundation of her faith the mysterious doctrines of predestination and election, which in Scripture are seldom mentioned but as topics of consolation and support to the tried and tempted believer; because she has marshalled her teaching, not according to artificial systems of men, but in simple conformity to the word of God.

If then,—to borrow an illustration from the present times,—we should think that the doctrine of holy baptism has been misunderstood or perverted, and should feel it our duty to explain or defend it, do not let us forget, that there are other doctrines as necessary to salvation and holiness; and that our Church has taught at least as dogmatically the truths of the Trinity, the Incarnation, and the Atonement; the inspiration of Holy Scripture, and its sufficiency as the rule of faith; original sin, and the infection of nature remaining after regeneration in which the guilt is remitted; the necessity of both preventing and co-operating grace; justification, or imputed righteousness, not for our own deservings but for the merits of our Lord and Saviour Jesus Christ by faith only, apart from works; the need of good works as the fruit and evidence of lively faith; and predestination to life, a doctrine of unspeakable comfort to the godly. All these, then, no less than the doctrines of the Church and sacraments, are "the things new and old" which we are to dispense faithfully and in due proportion accordingly as every one hath need; and we must take heed lest we keep back any of the counsel of God, if we would be free from the blood of all men.

Let me add, that to teach any doctrine exclusively, or to give it undue prominence, has a tendency to generate errors in the opposite extreme. There is a reaction from the overstrained statement even of truth. Points which *we* have neglected, are perceived by others. It becomes their duty to restore them to their due position. They soon exaggerate their importance. Opposition makes their defence warmer, their language stronger, and their opinions more hard, exclusive, and antagonistic. They deny, at length, the tenets of their opponents, and push their own beyond the bounds of Scripture ; and what was at first the rescue of neglected truth, becomes at last error and even heresy. I need not remind you, how the history of philosophy, as well as of heresies, is a kind of register of the oscillations of the human mind, swinging alternately from one extreme to the other: nor detain you with instances of the ebb and flow of opinion, which your own memory will readily supply even from the annals of our own Church. But let us, taught by experience, " take heed to our doctrine," lest by the too exclusive teaching of even important truth we prepare the way for the revival and reception of opposite error: lest, for instance, by undue or exaggerated statements of the doctrine of sacramental grace we should be provoking a speedy recoil to a miserable rationalism, or the cold, faithless heresy of Socinus.

2. And this leads me to mention one more danger, to which our teaching is exposed in times of controversy. It is that of neglecting, in our interest in the questions of the day, the growth of other errors often more formidable and deadly. While our eyes are fixed on the contest in front, the enemy is undermining the walls or attacking the rear. Never surely was the warning more needed. All know the questions which agitate the Church. The press teems with them; the platform rings with them. They are

discussed daily, even by those who ought not, and in tones very unbefitting sacred truth. But is this the quarter where our people's danger lies? Is it here that errors are generating, which are already poisoning the faith especially of the young? Can we be blind to the signs of the times exhibited in the popular literature of the day? or disguise from ourselves that the Church must prepare to combat the resuscitated heresies of the first two centuries, armed with the science and mental acuteness of the nineteenth? The inspiration of Scripture, the origin of evil, the eternity of punishment, the resurrection of the body, the personality of the evil spirit,—all these are questions on which the minds of men are at work, and on which opinions the most pernicious to Christianity, and indeed to natural religion, are festering in the bosom of society. Add to this a growing rationalistic spirit with its self-conceited criticism, erecting the individual feeling and judgment,—the I myself,—into the standard of right and wrong, truth and falsehood, and thus reaching by a widely differing road the ultimate conclusions of mysticism; and the difficulties which the results of modern science are supposed and taught to have raised to revelation, and which, where they have not led to infidelity, have induced a wide-spread sentiment, that there are many things in the Bible which need not be believed, and have consequently furnished a ready plea for rejecting or passing over whatever is distasteful to the pride of intellect or the erring will. Nor can we forget the less dangerous, perhaps, because more daring, efforts of the Roman Church, now elated to new hope by the faithlessness, alas! or the weakness of some from among ourselves; and who has at length ventured to assume again a long-lost authority, the exercise of which involves the denial, on Rome's principles, and indeed on our own, of the existence of our Episcopacy, the validity of our orders, and the efficacy of our sacraments.

These are "erroneous and strange doctrines contrary to God's word" which are rapidly rising around us, and which we are vowed "with all faithful diligence to banish and drive away." Let us "take heed," then, "to ourselves and unto the doctrine;" and be prepared to guard on all sides the flock committed to our charge.

And that we may do so, oh let us pray more earnestly, and endeavour more sincerely, to be at peace among ourselves. Let us not exaggerate differences, impute motives, or multiply parties; but rather let us rejoice to agree in great points, and agree to differ in less. Let not verbal disputes become real divisions; nor let us charge each other with disowning doctrines, which we alike profess. Rather let us "believe all things, hope all things, endure all things."[1] When the enemy surrounds the camp, disunion is treason; union alone is safety.

[1] 1 Cor. xiii. 7.

One in heart, and one in effort, we shall soon find ourselves one in sentiment: and a united band of brethren, fighting under Christ's own banner, we are secure of the victory through the might of our own great Head, the Captain of our salvation.

THE END.

G. NORMAN & SON, Printers, Maiden Lane, Covent Garden.

www.ingramcontent.com/pod-product-compliance
Lightning Source LLC
Chambersburg PA
CBHW021820230426
43669CB00008B/818